The Pueblo Zoo Through the Years

An Inside Look

Jonnene D. McFarland
Martha M. Osborn

Copyright © 2019 Jonnene D. McFarland and Martha M. Osborn

All rights reserved. No part of this publication may be reproduced, stored in a retrieval system, or transmitted, in any form or by any means, electronic, mechanical, photocopying, recording or otherwise, without the prior written permission of the authors.

Jonnene D. McFarland and Martha M. Osborn assert the moral right to be identified as the authors of this work.

Publisher's Cataloguing-in-Publication data

Names: McFarland, Jonnene D. [Jonnene Irene Dunlop] | Osborn, Martha M.
Title: The Pueblo Zoo Through the Years: An Inside Look
Description: Palm Springs, California : Old John Publishing, 2019 |
Identifiers: LCCN 2019909213| ISBN 978-0-9976809-6-6 (hardcover)/
    978-0-9976809-7-3 (softcover)
Subjects: LCSH : Zoo–History–Pueblo | Colorado–History, Local–20th
    Century
Classification : LCC QL76.5.U.65 M164 2019
LC record available at https://lccn.loc.gov/2019909213

References to Internet Web sites (URLs) were accurate at the time of writing. Neither the author nor Old John Publishing is responsible for URLs that may have expired or changed since the manuscript was prepared.

Dedicated to our families who supported our work
with their encouragement, patience, and love.

<u>Osborns</u>
Neal Osborn
Christi, Mike, Matt, and Katie Kurtz
Kelton, Sarah, and Gwendolyn Osborn

<u>McFarlands</u>
Jennifer, Andy, Lauren, and Hannah Whisman
Jeanne, Steven, Katy, and Jack McDonald
Janet, Cory, and Ruby Burlile

In memory of
three dear friends
—Laura Mattoon, Art Schwager, and Marilyn McBirney—
without whom this story would not have been possible.

In honor of
the creativity of Richard Montano.

Animals depicted on the cover
(*clockwise from upper left*):

Africa Lion
American Bison
Crested Partridge
Emerald Tree Boa
Cotton-top Tamarin
African Penguin
Shama Thrush
Crested Porcupine
Sulawesi (Celebus) Macaque
Bengal Tiger
Andean Condor
Tomato Frog
Llamas
Hoffman's Two-toed Sloth
Blue and Gold Macaw
Red Panda
North American River Otters
Maned Wolf
Emu
Beisa Oryx
Rusty-spotted Cat
Rodrigues Island Fruit Bats
Bactrian Camel
Grizzly Bear

(*All cover images courtesy of the Pueblo Zoological Society*)

Contents

ACKNOWLEDGEMENTS	iii
INTRODUCTION	v
CHAPTER ONE: Early History: The Beginning Through 1975	1
CHAPTER TWO: The Middle Years: 1976 Through 1990	27
CHAPER THREE: From Fence to Fence: January 1991 to July 2012	51
CHAPTER FOUR: Animal House & Monkey Island Become Islands of Life	83
CHAPTER FIVE: Bringing Learning to Life	101
CHAPTER SIX: Fun, Friends, Fundraising	113
CHAPTER SEVEN: The Animals	125
CHAPTER EIGHT: The People	149
EPILOGUE: Retirement and Final Thoughts	163
APPENDIX A: Pueblo Zoological Society Board of Directors and Presidents, 1976 Through 2012	165
APPENDIX B: Pueblo Zoo Veterinarians, Early 1900s Through 2012	167
APPENDIX C: Tribute to Marilyn McBirney	171

Acknowledgements

We were privileged over our many years of working at the Pueblo Zoo to have known and to have worked alongside hundreds of fine people, and many of them are mentioned this book. Unfortunately, memories fade after so many years, particularly memories for names. Although we no doubt have left out many of those who contributed to the success of the Pueblo Zoo, please know that each and every one is nonetheless very much appreciated.

We owe a considerable debt to the late George R. Williams, who gave the Pueblo Zoological Society many priceless photographs and a wealth of information. We would also like to extend special thanks to the Pueblo County Historical Society for covering the costs of publishing this book; to our meticulous editors Mary Tucey, Janet McFarland Burlile, Distinguished Professor Emerita Marjorie McIntosh of the Department of History University of Colorado—Boulder, and to retired teacher of English Judy Pratt; to Abbie Krause, who became the Pueblo Zoo Director in 2015 and who provided important research assistance as well as copies of Pueblo Zoological Society newsletters and annual reports; to Barbara Lester and Paul Freed who, after Marilyn McBirney's death, sent us photographs from her collection; to Melanie Pococke, Heather Smith, Kim Cooper Pranger, Pat Ponce, Carol Rickman, and Sally Mara, who together helped us fill in many memory blanks; to Pat Ponce, Jeanette Ball, Janice Martinez, Verona Miller, Vivian Espinosa, Alice Olson, Verona Miller, Ilo Grisham, and Milt Kanzaki, each of whom through the years gathered newspaper articles, researched at the library, and kept the invaluable scrapbooks now stored in the Research Section of the Rawlings Library (Pueblo City-County Library District); and to Neal Osborn, Marti's patient husband, who endured snakes and a monkey living at their home, skulls boiling in their kitchen, and who was also Jonnie's advisor at the University of Southern Colorado (now Colorado State University, Pueblo).

In compiling the Pueblo Zoo's scrapbooks, publication information was sometimes omitted by the compilers from the local newspaper articles that they clipped. We therefore primarily cite *The Pueblo Chieftain*, although some of the articles may have been printed in its sister afternoon publication the *Star Journal* (1901-1984). Both newspapers were published by The Pueblo Chieftain & Star Journal Publishing Corporation.

All photographs , unless otherwise noted, are the property of and are used with the permission of the Pueblo Zoological Society. Any other photographs are used by permission of either the original photographer or the owner of the image.

All profits from the sale of this book have been pledged to the Pueblo Zoological Society Endowment Fund.

Introduction

> "It's a pretty good zoo,"
> Said young Gerald McGrew,
> "And the fellow who runs it
> Seems proud of it, too."
>
> "But if *I* ran the zoo,"
> Said young Gerald McGrew,
> "I'd make a few changes.
> That's just what I'd do . . ."
>
> *If I Ran the Zoo*, Dr. Seuss

This book chronicles the complex history of the Pueblo Zoo in Pueblo, Colorado. Starting with the Zoo's "triple" beginnings in three local parks, it traces the Zoo's development from its consolidation in City Park to the subsequent founding of the Pueblo Zoological Society and the beginning of the authors' own involvement in 1976, through the Zoo's transition to private management in 1991. It ends in the year of the authors' joint retirements from the Zoo in 2012. It is told from the authors' personal perspectives and relies heavily on personal memories, supplemented by the recollections of old-timers.

In the last few weeks before we, the authors, retired, we did considerable reminiscing, telling stories about the thirty-six years during which we had been associated with the Pueblo Zoo. Some of the stories were sad, some were happy, some revealed frustration, but many generated laughter from those listening. Friends and family members urged us to write a book about our experiences. And so we began what we thought would be only a few pages, but we got carried away. Those few pages of anecdotal stories rapidly evolved into the illustrated volume presented here.

The history of humans keeping zoos is a lengthy one dating back at least as far as the menageries of Ancient Egypt. It took zoos literally thousands of years to evolve into what are today's professionally managed institutions. That evolution within the United States moved much more rapidly, however, after the inception of the American Association of Zoos and Aquariums (AAZPA) in 1924 as a division of the National Recreation and Park Association. Then in 1971, and in response to mounting pressures for improvements in animal welfare, the AAZPA became an independent organization and quickly established a committee to formulate a set of best practices for zoo management. Zoo accreditation had been voluntary prior to 1974, but it became a requirement for membership in the AAZPA beginning in 1985. In 1994, the organization changed its name to the Association of Zoos and Aquariums (AZA). Today, zoos accredited by the AZA must meet the highest standards of animal care, strive to provide enjoyable family experiences, and dedicate themselves to the support of education, conservation, and scientific research.

Our involvement with the Pueblo Zoo began in the mid-1970s, a time when changes occurring nationwide, even worldwide, would have a great impact on the survival and future of the organization. If it was to survive, the Zoo had to meet not only state and federal standards but also the ever-increasing requirements for accreditation. The latter issue, that of accreditation, had a critical impact on animal acquisition and on the common practice of transferring surplus animals to other zoos, as only accredited facilities were allowed to receive such animals. At the same time, other changes of a more indirect nature, such as shrinking governmental funding, led an increasing number of zoos to become independent, privately managed, or overseen by public-private partnerships. Some communities even established independent taxing structures to support their zoos, such as Denver's Scientific and Cultural Facilities District or the St. Louis Metropolitan Zoological Park and Museum District. All of these issues had an effect on "our" little Zoo.

The qualifications required for zoo management personnel underwent significant changes as well. When we first started in the field, people trained in zoology managed most zoos. Many managers and directors had worked their way up the ranks from animal care positions. Denver Zoo Director Clayton Freiheit, for example, began his career as an animal caretaker at the Buffalo Museum of Science. Marlin Perkins, famous for his role in the television program *Mutual of Omaha's Wild Kingdom* in the 1970s, got his start as a reptile keeper before becoming director of the Buffalo, Lincoln Park, and St. Louis Zoos. But by about midway through our own careers, we began to observe a shift in this practice. Many zoos, driven by a need for increased revenues, were beginning to imitate the corporate world by choosing zoo directors and CEOs based on their business or marketing backgrounds rather than on the basis of any extensive knowledge of animal behavior and husbandry. Less apparent, perhaps, was the change from a previously male-dominated profession to one in which female workers are now employed at all levels. As we sought and hired experienced zookeepers, we found the Pueblo Zoo's animal care staff was becoming primarily female, as our administration already was. These are just some of the many changes affecting the Pueblo Zoo that are discussed in this volume.

Our history of the Pueblo Zoo begins long before either of us were born. It then moves to our own early years there, when we advocated for improvements, raised money to help make those improvements, and conducted an education program, all the while becoming increasingly frustrated with a lack of adequate progress. The third and fourth chapters chronicle the privatization of the Pueblo Zoo and the challenges presented by an associated drastic change in management. Chapters Five and Six detail specific activities and events undertaken by the Zoological Society. Chapter Seven tells the stories of a few of the most interesting animals that have resided at the Zoo. In Chapter Eight we introduce some of the people who for over a hundred years have cared for the Zoo and its animals. Appendix A offers a list of Presidents of the Board of Directors of the Pueblo Historical Society from its founding to 2012, while Appendix B lists the many dedicated veterinarians who worked at the Pueblo Zoo. Lastly, we pay tribute to our fellow senior staff member Marilyn McBirney in Appendix C.

It took a group of concerned citizens working together to transform a place they valued—the old City Park Zoo—into a nationally accredited zoo facility. Without the perseverance, enthusiasm, financial support, and loyalty of contributors, event sponsors, in-kind donors, grantors, advisors, honest contractors, clever designers, board members, docents, volunteers, dedicated employees, and government officials, the Pueblo Zoo probably would not have survived.

We hope you enjoy retaking the journey with us as we attempted to utilize our university degrees in biology in an unusual setting, yet learned so many things the hard way, and as we reminisce about so many old friends who helped us along the way.

In relating our illustrated history of the Pueblo Zoo, some of the photographs that we include in this book may depict Zoo staff, volunteers, and others in close contact with or holding animals. We freely acknowledge that the two of us, and indeed most of our fellow Zoo workers, did not know any better in those early years. After the Zoological Society assumed management, however, the Pueblo Zoo's staff and volunteers were required to adhere strictly to the Association of Zoos and Aquariums Ambassador Animal Policy, which states in part,

> An Ambassador Animal is defined as an animal whose role includes handling and/or training by staff or volunteers for interaction with the public and in support of institutional education and conservation goals. Some animals are designated as Ambassador Animals on a full-time basis, while others are designated as such only occasionally. Ambassador Animal-related Accreditation Standards are applicable to all animals during the times that they are designated as Ambassador Animals.[1]

The Pueblo Zoo's education program animals were primarily domestic animals rather than exotics and were designated as ambassadors on a full-time basis. In contrast, the Zoo's lion cubs born in 2006 were hand-raised only because they had been rejected by their mothers. They were handled only for a short time, from their birth until they were re-introduced to the adult lions.

---

[1] Association of Zoos and Aquariums, Animal Ambassador Policy, <www.aza.org/aza-ambassador-animal-policy>, updated January 2015, accessed 27 May 2019.

Chapter One

Early History:
The Beginning Through 1975

We begin our story of the Pueblo Zoo with an overview of its history from its founding to the eve of the incorporation of the Pueblo Zoological Society in 1976. The Pueblo Zoo originated in the late nineteenth century with small collections of animals apparently kept for the enjoyment of locals. But by the first years of the twentieth century, thought on the exhibition of animals had begun to evolve, led by what was called the "Hagenbeck Revolution" that transformed zoo exhibit architecture. Pueblo was able to join this revolution thanks to astute city management, which brought considerable funding from federal New Deal programs to the city in the wake of the Great Depression. But the outbreak of WWII pushed the Zoo into the historical background, with little information preserved to tell the story of those years. After the war, dedicated Parks Department employees made many improvements until the turbulent economy of the late 1960s and 1970s, together with the decline of steel production at Colorado Fuel and Iron in the early 1980s, unfortunately caused that progress very nearly to cease.

The First Park – Mineral Palace in Park District #1

The actual founding of the Pueblo Zoo evolved primarily out of the development early in the twentieth century of three public parks districts in the City of Pueblo. Each park district included pre-existing small collections of mostly local animals.[1] But the park districts devoloped in their turn from a prominent local landmark, the Colorado Mineral Palace, which had opened in Pueblo to much fanfare on July 4, 1891.[2] The Palace was designed to showcase Colorado's mineral wealth, and its grounds included Pueblo's first flower gardens. Inspired by the popularity of the Palace, and in response to the City Beautiful Movement then sweeping the US, the citizens of Pueblo soon began calling for a magnificent public park that would surround and complement the privately-held Palace. A plan developed by the Ladies Parks and Improvement Association (LPIA) and presented to the Pueblo Chamber of Commerce in 1896 actually called for four parks districts within the city, rather than one. Public Park District #1 was to include the Mineral Palace plus additional

---

[1] George R. Williams, "A Little Pueblo City Park Zoo Trivia," *The Pueblo Lore* 40:10 (October 2014), 14-16.
[2] The unheated building was poorly built and began to deteriorate within a year. By 1943, the Mineral Palace had been torn down for safety reasons and in order to provide metal for the war effort. Some of the wood from the building was stored at the City Park Zoo and later used to build corrals there.

surrounding land that would be developed for public use. Property owners subsequently approved a bond measure on August 2, 1897 for the establishment of the city's first park, to be known as Mineral Palace Park. Among its many amenities could be found a "zoological garden with tropical plants and trees. There was an animal zoo and children's playground."[3] The small Mineral Palace Park animal zoo formed the embryo from which the much larger Pueblo Zoo would eventually grow.

Pronghorn at the Mineral Palace Park Zoo in 1905.
(Image courtesy of John Suhay Historical Collection,
Pueblo City-County Library District)

---

[3] Anonymous, *History of Mineral Palace Park*, <https://www.pueblo.us/DocumentCenter/View/675/History-of-Mineral-Palace-Park> accessed May 11, 2019. See also "Colorful Colorado: Story of Pueblo's Mineral Palace," *The Pueblo Chieftain*, August 2, 1970.

The Second Park – City Park in Park District #2

The Pueblo Zoo would eventually develop in City Park rather than in Mineral Palace Park, however. City Park was to be located in Public Park District #2, and the land that constitutes that park has the longest documented history. It originally formed part of the Rock Canyon Ranch, where Charles and Molly Goodnight lived for six years after their marriage in 1870.[4] The historic Goodnight barn still stands near the Arkansas River just a short distance west of the Zoo.

Goodnight sold his ranch late in the 1870s, and the land was owned in the 1880s by the Colorado Coal and Iron Company (CCIC). In 1889, a group of South Pueblo investors purchased a 150-acre parcel of the land from the CCIC. Charles Dittmer served as General Manager for the investment group, with the responsibility of establishing an elite suburban area to include the "Park" as well as an adjoining housing development. Born in Sweden and successful in mining and railroads, Dittmer was a practical person with an appreciation for art, design, and horticulture, and the "Park" soon reflected those influences. He built fountains and lakes and planted more than 70 varieties of trees and shrubs to create a mosaic of color and texture in pleasant patterns of growth during all seasons.[5]

Charles Goodnight, ca. 1880[6]

Although the Silver Crash of 1893 affected many Pueblo area projects, Dittmer and his partners survived that economic crisis until the Panic of 1903 forced them to dispose of the "Park" parcel. In that year, because Southside residents wanted a public park comparable to the one constructed around the Mineral Palace, Southside property owners approved a $175,000 bond issue to purchase the parcel from Dittmer and his partners. Thirty acres were specifically designated for a public zoo.[7] Public Park District #2, located west of the city and south of the Arkansas River, was approved in 1903, and City Park was opened in 1904.

---

[4] As a cattleman, Charles made numerous hazardous cattle drives along the Goodnight-Loving Trail that ran from Texas to Wyoming. He must have been quite a character as well, since it was reported that he smoked 50 cigars a day, and after Molly's death in 1926—and on his own 91st birthday—Charles married his paternal first cousin, a 27-year-old nurse named Corinne Goodnight. She subsequently miscarried a child by the nonagenarian Charles. For a full accounting of the life of Charles Goodnight, see J. Evetts Haley, *Charles Goodnight: Cowman and Plainsman*, rev. ed. (Norman: University of Oklahoma Press, 1981) or William T. Hagen, *Charles Goodnight: Father of the Texas Panhandle* (Norman: University of Oklahoma Press, 2011).

[5] George R. Williams, "The History of City Park," <https://www.pueblo.us/DocumentCenter/View/671/The-History-of-City-Park>, 2002-2009, accessed May 11, 2019.

[6] Image reprinted from Hagen, *Charles Goodnight*.

[7] Williams, "The History of City Park."

Deer at Mitchell Park.
(*Image Courtesy of Wheat Collection, Pueblo City-County Library District*)

The Third Park—Mitchell Park in Park District #3

The LPIA plan of 1896 called for an additional park to overlook the entire city. Mitchell Park opened in 1902 on what was then the highest point in Pueblo. One of the pens at the park housed deer.[8]

The Pueblo Zoo Is Born

What is now the Pueblo Zoo was formally created in the wake of a visit to Pueblo in 1905 by Carl Hagenbeck of the Hagenbeck Shows. A German animal merchant, Hagenbeck is credited with the transformation of zoo architecture through the creation of more naturalistic habitats rather than barred cages, known as the "Hagenbeck Revolution" in zoo design. Hagenbeck wished to establish a zoo in the Rocky Mountain region, and Pueblo was looked upon as a site having many advantages.[9] But Pueblo did not immediately establish a central zoo based on Hagenbeck's ideas. Instead, three separate collections of mostly-local animals continued to grow within each of the three parks. A few interesting newspaper stories survive to provide us with some insights into those collections.

---

[8] Jeffrey DeHerrera and Charlene Garcia Simms, *Pueblo's East Side History and Heritage*, prepared for the History Wall at the Patrick A. Lucero Library, East Side Pueblo, Pueblo City-County Library District, 2014 and reproduced at <http://www.pueblolibrary.org/EastsideHistoryWall>, accessed May 11, 2019; Peter Roper, "Mitchell Park: The Heart of the East Side," *The Pueblo Chieftain*, June 9, 2003, 5A.

[9] "May Establish Zoo in Pueblo," *The Pueblo Chieftain*, November 22, 1905.

The principal local newspaper, *The Pueblo Chieftain*, first reported on the animals at Mineral Palace Park in 1908. It described two deer moved from Mitchell Park to the collection at Mineral Palace Park as, "very happy in their new home and [they] show it in scampering about the large enclosure and throwing their heads in the wind with a the-world-is-mine look." The Zoo's coyotes

> put up their blood curdling yelps every time a train passes the park, probably in an effort to let incoming passengers know they are in the wild and wooly west and to give outgoing passengers a farewell note of the west.[10]

Joe Fritzel Sr., who began caring for the animals at the Mineral Palace Park in about 1908, called it a "zoo of sorts." It was "less than adequate. A couple of eagles, owls, and bears and a scraggly coyote or two were caged there, but that was about it."[11]

The first addition at the City Park Zoo was

> grazing land for a few pasture animals—half dozen Colorado elk, five Colorado mule deer, three buffalo, and several antelope. Larger quarters were built near the park's center for a growing menagerie [and] additional grassland [was] planted. Then, still more cages became necessary, and a meat house was constructed behind the animal cage area.[12]

In 1920, *The Pueblo Chieftain* noted Commissioner James Lee Lovern's announcement that there would be monkeys in each of Pueblo's larger parks where "the youngsters and grownups, too, can enjoy themselves by throwing peanuts to the little animals." But Lovern also speculated that other animals then in Mitchell and Mineral Palace parks might be moved to the City Park Zoo where they would collectively receive better care without additional cost. Lovern mentioned deer, elk, buffalo, bears, owls, raccoons, pheasants, prairie dogs, rabbits, groundhogs, and porcupines residing in the three parks.[13]

More animals were added to the collection in City Park, with *The Pueblo Chieftain* reporting in 1923 that several elk had been obtained from Buena Vista. Elk and Siberian deer seemed to "lord it over the other animals," and the bison were described as "two huge hunks of flesh." Superintendent Colby said that the Siberian deer were the only ones in the country, having been brought to Pueblo directly from Russia by Charles Dittmer.[14] The elk herd was later rejuvenated through an exchange of animals with the Spencer Penrose Estate in Colorado Springs.[15]

The arrival of new animals sometimes created challenges for those who cared for them. The following story was relayed by the Chieftain in 1924 under the title "Brownie's Escapade in Mineral Palace Park."

> "Brownie," the larger of the two young bears in the zoo at Mineral Palace Park, got peeved Sunday and, with bear-like reasoning, … proceeded to separate C. W. Shaver from most of his wearing apparel. "Brownie" has put up with many … unreasonable demands of man … being a well-known figure in parades and stunts. Of late as he grew older he has become more and

---

[10] "An Interesting Zoo at Mineral Palace," *The Pueblo Chieftain*, January 21, 1908.
[11] "Family Tradition of Animal Care," *The Pueblo Chieftain*, April 6, 1971.
[12] "Family Tradition of Animal Care," *The Pueblo Chieftain*, April 6, 1971.
[13] "Big Zoo Contemplated for City Park; Large Number of Animals Owned by City," *The Pueblo Chieftain*, February 8, 1920.
[14] It is not clear from the article as to which of the several species of deer native to Siberia is intended.
[15] "One Man Had Much to do with Planning Two Parks," *The Pueblo Chieftain*, January 21, 1924.

more disinclined to submit to all the demands made upon him—getting hard to handle. So, the decision was made to place a ring in his nose. ... This ring-in-the-nose business failed to appeal at all to "Brownie" and in the scuffle that accompanied the first attempts to disfigure his honeyfinder [sic] he used his claws, Shaver being the object of his attention. The man's clothes were all but torn from his body, and he suffered numerous scratches. Sleep-producing potions were then used on Brownie, and man's will prevailed.[16]

The "New Deal" Impacts the Zoo

The area of Southwestern Colorado that includes the City of Pueblo suffered economically during the Great Depression, like most of the US, but both the city and its Zoo benefited from Franklin Roosevelt's "New Deal" program for national economic recovery. Hundreds of Pueblo's men found themselves unemployed after the stock market crash of 1929. The City had been a major manufacturing center, but that sector of Pueblo's economy was paralyzed by the Great Depression. The issue was compounded by drought, dust storms that lasted for days, and plagues of grasshoppers that devastated the local agricultural economy. Colorado looked for assistance from the federal programs that were part of the "New Deal" and was not disappointed. Between 1933 and 1940, the Civilian Conservation Corps (CCC), the Colorado Works Administration (CWA), the Public Works Administration (PWA), and the Works Progress Administration (WPA)—to name a few of the programs—funded construction of roads, bridges, schools, government buildings, parks, and many other public improvements while providing work for about 60,000 unemployed. What would become known as the Pueblo Zoo benefited from the "New Deal" program due primarily to the efforts of one man, Raymond Herbert Talbot.

As the dominant political leader in Southern Colorado from 1926 until 1946, Talbot was a man of great vision. Though born in Chicago, he grew up from the age of one year in Pueblo. He married Juniatta L. Wilson in 1915, and the couple had two children. He was successively elected Colorado State Representative, State Senator, and Lieutenant Governor, and for ten days served as Governor of Colorado, completing the term of Edward Johnson, who had been elected to the U. S. Senate. While serving as Lieutenant Governor in 1932, Talbot was additionally appointed Pueblo City Commissioner for Parks and Highways.[17] Under his leadership during the Great Depression, the City of Pueblo felt its way through early work relief programs. Consequently, when the WPA was established in 1935, the city was prepared to take full advantage of the program. By 1939, 113 construction and 10 non-construction projects had been completed locally at a total cost of just over $4 million—an impact to the Pueblo economy in today's dollars of over $65 million.

As a result of Ray Talbot's foresight and political action, laborers funded by the "New Deal" began to build a state-of-the-art zoo in City Park, with much of the design based on the ideas of Hagenbeck's Revolution. Several barred cages were constructed first, followed by the Bear Pits, the Tropical Birdhouse, the miniature Monkey Mountain, a barn for hay storage,

---

[16] "When Brownie Becomes Peeved Things Happen Fast at the Zoo," *The Pueblo Chieftain*, April 21, 1924.

[17] "Colorado Governors: Raymond H. Talbot," <https://www.colorado.gov/pacific/sites/default/files/Talbot.pdf>, undated, accessed May 11, 2019.

CWA & WPA supervisors, 1934.
Raymond H. Talbot stands at the center of the front row.
(*Image courtesy of the Reeves Collection, Pueblo City-County Library District*)

Monkey Island, the Animal House, and lastly a moat to surround hoofed animal pens.

A large structure containing several heavily barred cages was moved from Mineral Palace Park to City Park in 1933. The following year, workers employed by CWA Project 17 built additional new cages on both ends of the relocated ones.

The cages used at City Park prior to 1935 to house the bears that had been transferred from Mineral Palace Park proved inadequate in terms of both compliance with the philosophy of Hagenbeck's Revolution and with the need for secure containment. In 1934, one intrepid bear managed to escape her cage.

> Maud, one of the [black bears] housed in the barred cages moved to the City Park Zoo from the Mineral Palace Park in 1933, went visiting at City Park Sunday evening. Before she returned home, police were called to make certain she would. She climbed to the top of her cage ... and managed to work herself over the sharp-pointed guard railing on top of steel bars. She walked around on the railing for a brief time, and then ... slid down the bars into the adjoining coyote cage. Maud placidly returned home when Theo P. Hamilton opened a door between the two cages.[18]

---

[18] "Bear Crawls Out of Cage at City Park — Fun Begins," *The Pueblo Chieftain*, June 1, 1936.

The CWA Project 17 workers who constructed the barred cages.
(*Image courtesy of the Reeves Collection, Pueblo City-County Library District*)

The completed line of barred cages as they appeared on March 26, 1934.
(*Image courtesy of the Reeves Collection, Pueblo City-County Library District*)

Bears in one of the cages moved from Mineral Palace Park.
(*Image courtesy of Pueblo City-County Library District*)

Work on the Bear Pits began in 1935. The four long, below-ground-level stone pits measured a total of 9,600 square feet. WPA workers dug the massive hole by hand and then created dramatic rock walls.

Construction of the Bear Pits began at the east end. The small building seen in the background at the upper right (circled) was called the "meat house" and was where food for the animals was stored and prepared.

(*Photograph by R.A. Merz, used courtesy of Pueblo Zoological Society collection*)

A zookeeper stands with two bears in one of the pits.

(*Image courtesy of the Wheat Collection, Pueblo City-County Library District*)

Two young bears climb a tree in the Bear Pits.

(*Image courtesy of the Wheat Collection, Pueblo City-County Library District*)

In August 1935, Congress approved a WPA program for Pueblo that allocated $23,000 to build a Tropical Bird House at the Zoo. Built of rough-hewn mountain surface stone hauled from a quarry thirty miles from the city, it was cooled by water trickling down the stones in nine cages and ending in a pond for ducks in the cage at the east end. In 1936, deer were traded for birds from California and Texas to fill the cages. It is interesting to note the wide variety of birds included: Bahamian tree ducks; ring-necked doves; native black birds; blue mountain lories; African and dwarf Mexican parrots; sacred white, bleeding heart, and native turtle doves; Nyasaland African, mask face, and peach face parakeets; Mexican red, pope, and crested Brazilian cardinals; orioles; cobalt, white, green, and yellow shell love birds; canaries; finches; sage hens; pheasants; grouse; and peacocks. In addition, white-faced ringtail monkeys were exhibited.[19]

WPA workers in front (south) of the completed Tropical Bird House.

(*Photograph by R. A. Merz, used by courtesy of the Pueblo Zoological Society collection*)

The south face of the Tropical Bird House.

(*Image courtesy of the Wheat Collection, Pueblo City-County Library District*)

[19] Simon Elliot, "A Home Worthy of the Proudest Birds and Beasts," *Pueblo City Guide*, January 28, 1938.

Monkey Mountain

Work began on a 37-foot "mountain" in 1933, in part with earth excavated from the adjacent Bear Pits. The mountain followed no definite design—it simply grew. WPA workers completed its massive stone walls in 1936, with a reservoir to provide a watershed for the small rivers and waterfalls that ran down its north face, plus trails. A beaver pond on the western side was stocked by the State Game Department. It is believed that the mountain was intended to house deer, which could seek shelter in two caves at its base, but there is no evidence that it was actually used in this way. Known fondly and as early as the 1940s as "Monkey Mountain," it became a play area for children from throughout the city.

Construction begins on north side of Monkey Mountain.
(*Image courtesy of the Wheat Collection, Pueblo City-County Library District*)

Dirt from the Bear Pits piled against Mountain structure.
(*Image courtesy of the Wheat Collection, Pueblo City-County Library District*)

The WPA workers climbed up and down the mountain so many times each day that they gave it a permanent highway designation on a marker at the summit.
(*Image courtesy of the Reeves Collection, Pueblo City-County Library District*)

Monkey Mountain as it appeared soon after its completion.
In subsequent years, George R. Williams and a Parks Department crew
added dirt and rocks between the walls to prevent erosion.

(*Image courtesy of the Wheat Collection, Pueblo City-County Library District*)

New Deal projects continued at the Zoo. In 1938, workers used native limestone quarried in the area to build a large barn on the south side of the Zoo property. The barn was equipped with track pulleys and a hayfork system that allowed Parks Department employees to unload loose hay harvested from land west of the Zoo, to elevate it up to the track, and to carry the load to the interior of the building.

In 1959, the CCC barn was set on fire by a group of youths. City workers used building materials brought from an old hanger at the Pueblo Municipal Airport to replace the roof. Whether or not the youths were caught has been lost to history.[20]

---

[20] Adapted from George R. Williams' interview on August 3, 1993, National Register of Historic Places Application, Janet McFarland Burlile, 2000.

The newly-built barn in a photograph taken on February 8, 1938.
(*Image courtesy of the Reeves Collection, Pueblo City-County Library District*)

The barn shortly after the fire.
(*Image courtesy of the Pueblo City-County Library District*)

Construction of Monkey Island began in 1938 and was completed a year later. It was built to display monkeys during the summer. Surrounded by a concrete moat, the island featured a stone lighthouse complete with an operational light in its lantern room, a miniature shipwreck, and on the northeast corner the wooden "Old Man's Club" where the monkeys were fed fruit and vegetables. Because the workers were so fond of City Commissioner and WPA organizer Ray Talbot, they named the miniature shipwreck the *Ada Mae* after his daughter. Both the lighthouse and the *Ada Mae* provided the primates with climbing and exploring opportunities. The "Old Man's Club" was removed many years ago.

Monkey Island in the 1940s.
(*Image courtesy of the Wheat Collection, Pueblo City-County Library District*)

The shipwrecked *Ada Mae* in the 1940s.
(*Image courtesy of the Talbot Family*)

An article in *The Pueblo Chieftain* on March 4, 1939 announced that the City Park Zoo would be enlarged through the construction of a sizeable animal house and a moat to surround the entire Zoo.[21] The 6,720 square foot animal house, a $61,000 WPA project, was built adjacent to Monkey Island and provided winter quarters for the animals. The moat—9' deep, 20' wide, and half a mile long—replaced some of the fences around buffalo, deer, antelope, and monkey enclosures.

The Animal House was constructed in 1939 and 1940. The interior included fourteen animal cages decorated with brightly colored bas-reliefs and a sculptural public drinking fountain. The central rotunda contained a decorative pool featuring three shiny black seals and several smaller animals sculpted of concrete. The inner side of the cupola atop the rotunda was lined with what appears to be fiberboard insulation on which were painted colorful mosaics. The cages were fronted with bars permitting direct contact with the public. A bridge to the island connected with several cages along the east side of the building and allowed the monkeys housed there to move outdoors in good weather. Three life-size sculpted concrete animals—a lion, a gorilla, and a bear—stood atop the cupola while two carved monkeys flanked the entrance from the island into the building. Completion of the Animal House in 1940 marked the end of both WPA- and New Deal-sponsored construction at the Zoo.

This aerial photograph from 1941 shows some of the structures that were built in the City Park Zoo using New Deal funding.[22] Monkey Mountain can be seen near the center, with the four bear pits to the left and Monkey Island with its lighthouse to the lower right. The Tropical Bird House is to the left. The Animal House is hidden from view in this photograph.

(*Image courtesy of Glen Nichols, Pueblo Star Journal, Courtesy Joan Wolther*)

---

[21] "City Park Zoo to be Enlarged," *The Pueblo Chieftain*, March 4 1939.
[22] Today, five of the New Deal-funded structures survive and are listed on the National Register of Historic Places as the "Pueblo Zoo Historic District."

A small primate reaches through the bars to take an item from a human hand.
(*Image courtesy of the John Suhay Collection, Pueblo City-County Library District*)

A problem soon became apparent with the Animal House: the public could interact directly with the animals through the bars that fronted the cages. An article published in *The Pueblo Chieftain* in 1940 stated,

> A close watch is necessary to keep spectators from feeding burning cigarettes to the monkeys and to keep them from pulling the tails and fur of animals such as lions who, all too gentle for their own good, lie against the bars of their cages. ... The only animal that ever has hurt anyone is the spotted leopard, who is gentle enough when left alone, but quite vicious when tormented. He has injured several persons who insisted on reaching into his cage.[23]

A railing was installed in the years that followed in order to hold visitors away from the cages. Even later, the bars were replaced with glass.

After the start of World War II in 1941, the public's attention turned to the war effort and many New Deal workers became soldiers instead. New construction at the Zoo ceased. The local newspaper published few articles about the Zoo during the war years. But a near-tragedy was nonetheless reported in 1942.

> Monoxide gas fumes from a coal furnace in the basement of the animal house in City Park killed seven monkeys and seriously menaced the lives of 23 other monkeys and other animals of the City Park Zoo which are housed in the building during the winter months. The rescue squad of the fire department, directed by Chief J. J. Fitzpatrick and Dr. A. N.

---

[23] Interview of T. P. Hamilton by *The Pueblo Chieftain*, undated 1940, clipping in *Pueblo Zoo Album 1940 - 1970*, Rawlings Library, Pueblo City-County Library District.

Carroll, veterinarian, saved the rest of the monkeys by placing them in oxygen tents. The five lions, leopard, and six raccoons ... although dazed by the fumes, were not so badly affected. Park Commissioner Ray H. Talbot and George L. Williams, Park Superintendent, and zoo attendants removed the stricken animals from the building. Fire department exhaust fans were placed in the building ... and repairmen restored the furnace to service.[24]

The deceased monkeys were buried about 150 yards south of the "meat house." Years later, someone digging a ditch unearthed the bones. There was a great deal of excitement surrounding the possibility that they might be human bones, until the situation was clarified by the Parks Department.[25]

Policeman Earl Butler holds a monkey while (left to right) city carpenter Bernard Lefrich, zookeeper T.P. Hamilton, Fire Chief Jeff Fitzpatrick, fireman Bud Woods, and zookeeper Mack Whittemore watch.
(*Image courtesy of George R. Williams and Rawlings Library, Pueblo City-County Library District*)

---

[24] "Fumes Kill Seven Monkeys at City Park Zoo," *The Pueblo Chieftain*, undated clipping in *Pueblo Zoo Album 1940-1970*, Rawlings Library, Pueblo City-County Library District.
[25] Personal communication, George R. Williams.

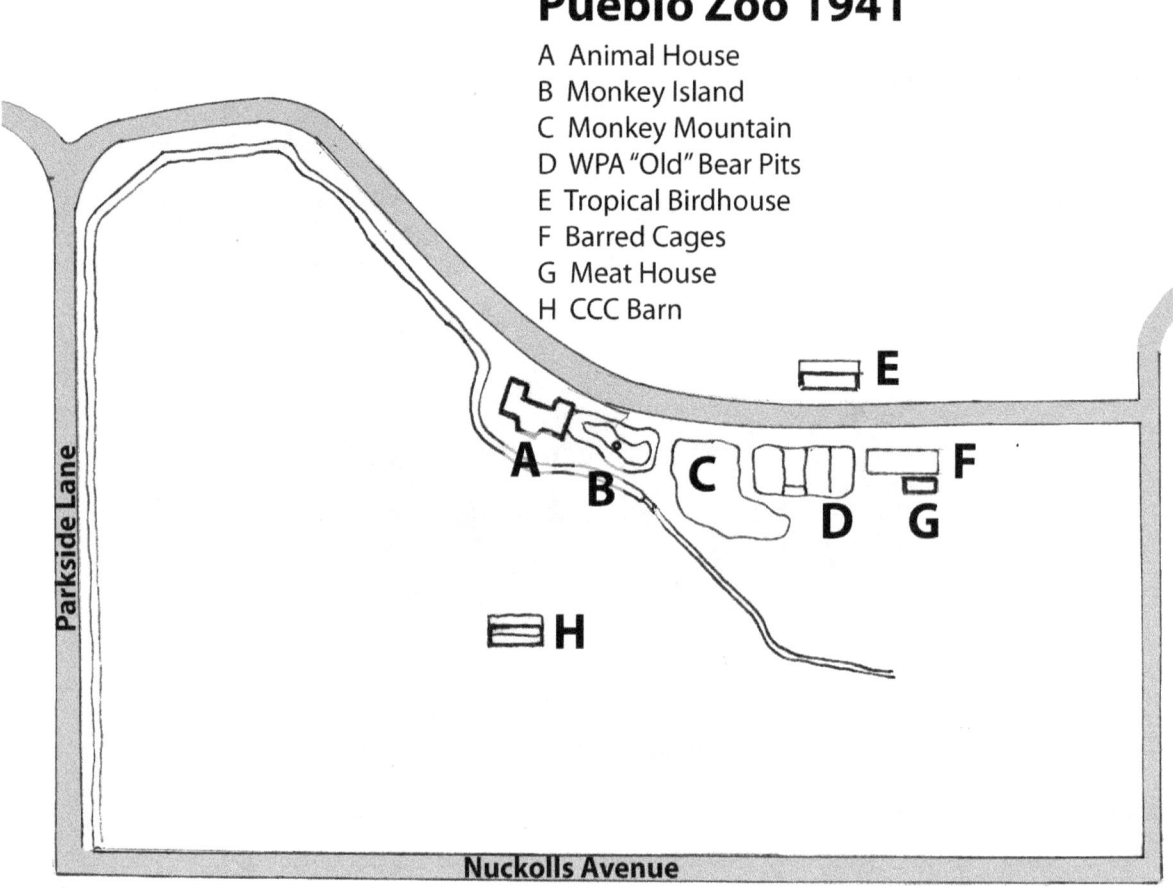

Map of the Pueblo Zoo layout as it appeared in 1941.
(*Drawing by Richard Montano drawing, legend by Steven McDonald*)

Happy Time Ranch in 1960.
(*Image courtesy of Earle W. Bodine & Pueblo County Historical Society*)

The 1950s and 1960s

Public interest in the Zoo revived in the 1950s. Early in that decade, George R. Williams toured the Denver Zoo and saw miniature farm buildings in a children's area. He later sent the Parks Department foreman and two caretakers to Denver to examine and measure the little structures. During the winter of 1958-59, using peeled logs from trees they harvested from the Ophir Creek drainage in the San Isabel National Forest and stones gathered from ranch lands in the Muldoon Hill and Goodpasture areas near Beulah, they built a barn, a blacksmith's shop, corrals, a house, and a privy complete with a Sears catalog. According to George L. Williams (George R.'s father), Director of the Parks Department, the total cost of the project was $1,000. It was paid to the Jones Saw Mill in Beulah for rough-sawn lumber for the window frames, doors, and roof sheathing, plus nails and also cement and sand for footings and floors. George R. Williams and his crew scoured the mountains near Pueblo in order to find genuine pioneer artifacts, including a hand-propelled grinding stone, a rusty fence stretcher, and a chicken-watering container that resembled a moonshiner's jug. These were used to provide an air of authenticity to the farm area. Plans called for burros, bantam

The miniature ranch house was complete with a dinner bell and an outhouse.
(*Image courtesy of the Pueblo County Historical Society*)

chickens, calves, and three little pigs to be housed in the farm. Carolyn Voss, wife of the Mayor at the time, chose the name Happy Time Ranch because she wanted "the children and adults to have a happy time when they come to see the baby animals."[26]

At the beginning of 1953, George L. Williams (George R.'s father) reported that 300,000 people had visited the City Park Zoo during the previous eight months. He listed the Zoo's inventory as

> three Philippine monkeys, three Java monkeys, two capuchin monkeys, one rhesus monkey, one spider monkey, two cinnamon ringtail monkeys, two white-faced monkeys, five coati mundis [sic], two hamsters, one badger, two California gray foxes, two Canadian silver foxes, one brown fox, four Colorado porcupines, four skunks, two raccoons, two bobcats, two Colorado eagles, one prairie hoot owl, seven white pigeons, seven peafowl, one emu, four African lions, three native mountain lions, three Colorado black bears, one Canadian brown bear, two Canadian black bears, five coyotes, 12 Japanese Sika deer, nine native mule deer, 18 white fallow or Siberian deer, five spotted fallow deer, and 130 ducks.[27]

---

[26] George R. Williams, "Additional Happy Time Ranch Information," *The Pueblo Lore* 36:1 (January, 2010), 7; Obituary for Caroline Cramer Voss, *The Pueblo Chieftain*, February 9, 2000.

[27] "300,000 Visit City Park Zoo," *The Pueblo Chieftain*, January 1, 1953.

Monkey Island and The Animal House in the 1950s.
(*Image courtesy of the Pueblo Zoological Society*)

In the late 1950s, the Parks Department renovated Monkey Mountain, replenishing dirt that had eroded away and adding about 120 tons of rock to build more stone steps and walkways. According to George R. Williams, no matter how fast the men carried stones up the mountain during the day, kids rolled them down at night. The City finally provided a crane to help the men build faster than the kids could tear down. The former beaver pond was in-filled with soil.

In the 1960s, an additional but smaller bear pit was built in the center of the Zoo. According to George R. Williams, the pit was designed by a Denver architect who was a friend of a City Council member. Those working at the Zoo were given no input. The inadequacy of the facility would become apparent in the years to come. This concrete pit was circular with five somewhat wedge-shaped enclosures that were floored with concrete, serviced through guillotine doors from a central hallway, and viewed by visitors from above.

Providing meat for the Zoo's carnivores always was a challenge. During WWII, regular shipments of horsemeat had been received from the Pace Ranch in Piñon, eleven miles north of town. Sometime in the early 1970s, however, the owners of the ranch stopped selling horsemeat to the Zoo due to what they considered excessive state and federal regulation. At that time, about 70 to 100 pounds of meat was being consumed each day by two lions, one leopard, two wolves, and five coyotes. To better meet the dietary needs of the animals, a large cooler at the "meat house" was converted into a freezer so that large shipments of horsemeat from Kansas could be stored for longer periods.[28]

[28] "Too Many Regulations—Supplier of Meat for City Zoo to Close Shop," *The Pueblo Chieftain*, January 11, 1973.

The overall condition of the Zoo began to suffer in the 1960s as widespread economic globalization negatively affected American steel manufacturers, including Colorado Fuel and Iron, Pueblo's primary employer. By the end of the decade, the city's economy had become further depressed in the wake of nationwide inflation. It became impossible for the City to provide adequate funding for animal care as a result of those wider conditions. At the same time, the ethical issues associated with keeping animals in captivity initiated a rapid change in zoos in general.

Despite various attempts to improve the Zoo, conditions continued to decline, causing citizens to protest. In one remarkable letter to the editor of *The Pueblo Chieftain*, a visitor from San Diego voiced her concern regarding the conditions she had witnessed during her visit to the Zoo.

> Recently I took my five children to the City Park. We admired the beautiful trees and lush grass as we drove through. Little were we aware of the horrors awaiting us at the "zoo." The chimpanzee was dragging a tumor that was as big as a basketball. The leopard can take only six steps in any direction. The lions have given up trying to exercise since the cages are no more than six feet by four feet. I can't possibly express how much the zoo appalled me. The stench brought tears to my eyes, or was it man's inhumanity to animals carried to such a great extent? Please sell or give these animals to a zoo that can take care of them if it is impossible to house them properly. Have you no compassion for these creatures? We then took a stroll to the Happy-time Ranch. The idea is a very good one, but again we met with unclean and crowded conditions. In one cage with a wire bottom and no sand box were three kittens. Their food consisted of one pan of sour milk and a rusty pan of water. The crowning blow came when the children went to the restroom. These are very easy to find since you can follow your nose from anywhere in the park. The men's restroom has no sink and most of the windows are broken. When the door to the women's restroom is opened, one is reeled back on her heels from the stench. Right between these two accommodations the concession stand is located. Shades of nausea! Where is the Public Health and Humane Society? Get your heads out of the sand and go visit the zoo![29]

At about the same time, local university student Len Gregory mounted a campaign to get more space for the lions.[30] Consequently and in an attempt to address these conditions, a $250,000 bond issue for a new feline building in the northwest corner of the Zoo was put before the voters in 1969.[31] Unfortunately, it failed. Within a couple of years, however, the Pueblo City Council allocated funds to construct two larger indoor cages connected to additional outdoor cages for use by the lions. The indoor cages were fronted with glass, while those outdoors were barred.

> Work will start Monday on enlarging quarters for the three African lions at the controversial City Park Zoo Animal House, according to Fred Weisbrod, City Manager. ... Cramped conditions at the feline house have been the target of numerous protests. ... City Council allocated $10,000 from the 1971 budget for the project. The new cages, each about 10-by-20 feet, will be constructed in the south portion of the building ... and, later, outside caged areas

---

[29] Mrs. R. D. Springer of San Diego, CA, *The Pueblo Chieftain*, undated clipping in *Pueblo Zoo Album 1940-1970*, Rawlings Library, Pueblo City-County Library District.

[30] Gregory went on to work for *The Pueblo Chieftain* for 37 years, achieving the post of Executive Editor before leaving in 2001.

[31] "City Park Zoo Project Envisioned," *The Pueblo Chieftain*, October 27, 1969.

will connect with each. The lions currently are housed, along with a leopard, in small 6.5-by-8-foot cages on the west wing of the building.[32]

Sometime in the late 1960s or early 1970s, seven or eight additional hoofstock pens were built along the south perimeter of the Zoo using chain-link fencing material. Long-time City Manager Fred Weisbrod had recently visited the Lee Richardson Zoo in Garden City Kansas, which was at that time a free, "drive-through" facility with the majority of the exhibits able to be viewed from a public road. Weisbrod evidently brought the idea home to Pueblo. New pens were constructed so that the animal shelters within them had an open side that faced south towards Nuckolls Avenue. The public were then able to drive directly up to the fences so that they could view the animals from their cars, even when the animals were under shelter. The open sides of the shelters in the pens along the western perimeter of the Zoo already faced west, toward Parkside Lane, thus already allowing for the public to view the animals from that roadway as well. Also in the 1970s, the Parks Department improved the Zoo by using funds from the Federal General Revenue Sharing program to tear down the barred bears cages and, in another area of the Zoo, to build ponds and islands for waterfowl.

Despite the changes made in the previous two decades, by the late 1970s it was becoming apparent that the Zoo's future was in question and that many years of uncertainty lay ahead. Fortunately, there was a small group of Pueblo citizens willing to tackle the work and to make the changes that would be necessary to save their Zoo.

---

[32] "Cage Area at Zoo Will Be Enlarged," *The Pueblo Chieftain*, July 3, 1971.

Chapter Two

The Middle Years:
1976 through 1990

The "middle years" to which the title of this chapter refers are those when we, the authors, first became associated with the Pueblo Zoo. Marti landed a job with the Parks Department and brought her activist spirit with her to the job. Jonnie, unable to stand having her children see the animals kept in such poor conditions, joined Marti in advocating for improvements, developing and presenting animal education programs, raising money, and—in the opinion of the Parks Department officials and the Zoo's four City-employed zookeepers—causing trouble. Neither stayed within the assumed boundaries of their positions, whether volunteer or employee. Both pushed too hard and suffered reprimands. The newly formed Zoological Society provided the tools for raising funds and official advocacy, as well as supportive Board members always willing to pack a City Council meeting or to lend a shoulder to cry on.

The Pueblo Zoo in 1976

Before we describe how each of us found our way to the Zoo, we must begin with a description of the place as we found it in 1976. Although it was beloved by many, the local newspaper described what was then still called the City Park Zoo as "dreary if not inhumane."[1] The passage of time plus budget cuts had taken their toll. Four zoo keepers aided by a handful of teenaged summer workers and occasionally by other City departments struggled to keep it running. There was no fence, and so the property was accessible all day and all night. The facility did not generate basic revenue because there was no admission fee. Only one animal exhibit had a sign identifying the animal, and that was "African Lion."

Peter Batten, former director of the San Jose Zoo, described the condition of the City Park Zoo in 1976 in his book *Living Trophies – A Shocking Look at the Conditions in America's Zoos*.

> Pueblo: Uneaten Zupreme everywhere inside cat/monkey house. European bear very thin, neurotic; labeled "KILLER." Dingo pit full of debris, garbage, dirty water. Hawks housed with owls. General run-down condition for all exhibits. Saw no keepers anywhere in zoo. Drive-through arrangement for ungulate viewing, plus car parking in front of exhibits poor. No security—dogs and other animals can enter zoo.

---

[1] "Newly Formed Society: Upgrading of Inhumane Zoo, *The Star Journal*, August 30, 1976.

Capuchin monkeys on the *Ada Mae* play with a can floating in the Monkey Island moat that was overgrown with algae in 1976.

(*Image courtesy of the Pueblo Zoological Society*)

> The large monkey island with 10-foot moat is marred by a lighthouse and concrete boat in a shipwrecked condition. (It would be advantageous to the public and a kindness to the animals if a larger boat could be provided for the inhabitants which might embark on a one-way voyage—past the lighthouse—and out to sea.)[2]

Similarly, a letter from Fred Foster of Pueblo addressed to the editor of *The Pueblo Chieftain* described the New Bear Pits in a sarcastic tone.

> My brother has just left after a brief visit to Pueblo. He wants everyone to know he was impressed by something he saw here. ... I am referring to the newly constructed bear pits at the City Park Zoo. He admires the straightforward concept of putting animals into their place. ... No pretending to care about the animals that live in the zoo. ... He hopes nobody will destroy the integrity of the animal display by adding things like water, shade, grass, trees or anything that would cause the display to lose its unique character.[3]

It started in 1976 when Marti's children were growing up, and she was looking for something to do outside the home—something that would allow her to use her biology and education degrees. She went to the Parks Department and had a chat with Acting Director George R. Williams. He offered her a part-time job, saying, "Do something with the Zoo." What an open-ended charge!

Something had to be done if the Zoo was to survive. People needed to be organized, and improvements had to be made. Marti, hired to "do something with the Zoo," was the person chosen

---

[2] Peter Batten, *Living Trophies – A Shocking Look at the Conditions in America's Zoos* (New York: Thomas Y. Crowell Company, 1976), 198.
[3] Fred Foster, Letter to the Editor, *The Pueblo Chieftain*, November 14, 1976.

to lead the effort to found a zoological society and to begin an education program.

The initial meeting to organize the Pueblo Zoological Society was held in August of 1976. A newspaper article highlighted the challenges faced by the newly-formed Society.

> Upgrading Pueblo's City Park Zoo—long viewed by many as a dreary if not inhumane area for the display of creatures—is the target of a thrust by the newly created Pueblo Zoological Society. The Zoological Society was formed by a group of citizens concerned about the welfare of the animals and the future status of the Pueblo Zoo. ... A zoo can no longer play the role of a freak show, but if exhibits are properly designed to show animals as vital beings, who have their place in this world, they could become educational enrichment for children and adults, who visit it. It can also be a vital link, if it is used for the protection and salvation of endangered animals, as are many of the great zoos of the world.[4]

Soon after the first meeting of the Zoological Society, Marti took a brief tour of the zoo, mostly by car, and parked in front of the Animal House. Upon entering the building, she immediately noticed the peeling paint and thought, "Aha, I'll get a group of volunteers to paint the cages!" After obtaining permission from the Parks Department, she gathered her friends Karen Adams, Judy Alsever, Carol Chimento, Sondra Biddle, and Laura Mattoon, and the group got to work. They alerted the newspaper to the project, and a photograph in *The Pueblo Chieftain* was all that was needed to begin their long journey toward improving the "City Park Zoo."

In response to the publication of the photograph, a letter to the Zoological Society from the Pueblo Beautiful Association (PBA) said,

> The PBA recognizes an outstanding individual, business, or organization when they have helped improve the physical appearance of the community. The PBA presents its good citizenship award for the month of June to the Pueblo Zoological Society for their participation in painting the animal cages at City Park.[5]

Jonnene (Jonnie) McFarland's family moved to Pueblo in the fall of 1973. The next summer, she took her three daughters to City Park to see the Zoo. They came first to several barred cages, which they found to be awful! All that Jonnie can recall seeing were a couple of mangy bears in filthy cages, without shade or food. She did not let her girls go beyond those first cages. She instead took them home after buying snacks and drinks at the concession stand, which was at that time in the center part of the 1930s Tropical Bird House. Then sometime early in 1977, Jonnie met Marti at a social hour after a Sunday church service. Marti told Jonnie how she was establishing a zoological society to help improve the Zoo and invited Jonnie to attend a meeting. That first meeting featured a talk by a fellow with the biggest snake that Jonnie had ever seen! Finding the snake, the people, and the program all interesting, she joined the new zoological society and volunteered to serve as a docent.

During its first year, the growing Zoological Society achieved several important milestones. With the help of Zoo supporter and attorney Bill Mattoon, the organization was incorporated as a 501(c)3 non-profit. The Society also opened its first bank account, developed an advertising and

---

[4] "Newly Formed Society: Upgrades of Inhumane Zoo Is Good", *The Star Journal*, August 30, 1976.
[5] Pueblo Zoo Album 1976-1987, Rawlings Library, Pueblo City-County Library District.

The Zoological Society's first logo.
(*Image courtesy of the Pueblo Zoological Society*)

marketing logo, initiated a newsletter, sent out its first direct-mail solicitation seeking community support, and started a zoo library through the purchase of the first book.

The Zoological Society met in the offices of the Parks Department, with new people joining each month. A recurring theme of concern voiced repeatedly at the early meetings of the Society was, "Something needs to be done about the bear pits." By this was meant primarily the New Bear Pits located in the center of the Zoo. Built in the 1960s, the circular concrete-block structure was situated somewhat lower than ground level and was divided into five separate concrete-lined exhibits. They held a polar bear, a sun bear, a hyena, and a black bear. The fact that there was absolutely no shade for the animals posed a major concern. Several Society members therefore met with the Parks Department administrators, who agreed to install shade cloth over each pit. Soon thereafter, zookeepers and Society volunteers added logs, dirt, and other items to help keep the animals from being bored. The public was happy, at least for the time being.

Following success in making a few limited changes to the New Bear Pits, the Zoological Society shifted its concern to the Zoo's original bear pits constructed under the Works Progress Administration and known by the 1970s as the Old Bear Pits. A system of bars formed a barrier along the side of the pits normally used by visitors, but the other three sides lacked sufficient barriers and could easily be accessed by anyone willing to "break the rules." The Society discussed the lack of full safety barriers that completely surrounded the pits, but lengthy deliberations initially failed to produce a solution. Finally, in the wee hours of a December night in 1977, a 15-year-old boy attempted to retrieve coins from the floor of the pits, where they had fallen after

Laura Mattoon peers down on a grizzly bear.
Note the conspicuous absence of a security barrier.

(*Image courtesy of the Pueblo Zoological Society*)

being thrown at the animals by visitors. He bypassed the existing limited safety barriers, climbed down into one of the pits, and petted the grizzly bear. The bear knocked him down, bit his head, and carried him to the rear of the pit. Another boy tossed a trashcan into the pit and startled the bear, causing it to release the youth. The boy used the brief distraction to climb a tree. Police and firemen were called, and they used a ladder to bridge the distance between the pit wall and the tree. A firefighter then crawled across to rescue the profusely bleeding lad, who was later treated at Parkview Hospital. The Parks Department Director was quoted as blaming the incident on years of pranks and harassment of the animals. Very soon thereafter, the City had a new fence installed around the back and sides of the Old Bear Pits.[6]

The Zoological Society made every effort in its early years to work cooperatively with the Parks Department in order to address a variety of concerns about the Zoo. But the Society's relationship with the Parks Department was often like a roller coaster ride, with the Parks Department encouraging and praising the Society's efforts one day, then criticizing and berating the Society the next day. When the Society advocated new ideas and new ways of doing things, the Parks

---

[6] "Teen Injured by Grizzly After Venturing into Pit," *The Pueblo Chieftain*, December 25, 1977.

Department too often labeled those suggestions as interference. But throughout this period, the public continued to express concern about conditions for the animals. Letters to the editor of the local newspaper provided a forum for people to put their concerns before the public. One such letter from Mr. and Mrs. V. Vanell of Colorado Springs drew attention to the plight of the animals at the Zoo.

> The purpose of this letter is to bring to your readers' attention a sad situation noticed recently while visiting your City Park Zoo. The problem is in regard to the small area the lions and tigers are housed in. The expressions on these animals' faces tell the viewer many things. I am sure this is not the first complaint in behalf of these animals and I hope there are enough caring and concerned people in your city who will join forces and see what can be done to improve this matter. A line to … the Humane Society of the United States, … reporting this and asking for suggestions on how conditions could be improved might be informative and worthwhile. Animals are at the mercy of men and so many have had too little of it for so long a time. Think about it …. We hope that the next time we visit your lovely park and zoo we can feel better if housing has been improved for the lions and tigers.[7]

An article in the same paper and at about the same time likewise noted the poor conditions at the Zoo. The article described a Kodiak bear that had suffered a cut tendon from stepping on a beer bottle cap. Zoo Veterinarian W. D. "Butch" Carroll said of the incident, "There were no treatment rooms onsite, consequently had the bear not stopped bleeding, treatment would have required it be tranquilized and possibly moved. [But] malicious cruelty to animals is the biggest problem we have at the Pueblo Zoo." Parks Director Lew Quigley explained that glass had to be installed on the monkey and lion cages in order to stop so many things being thrown into their cages. Zoo records indicated that waterfowl were mutilated, a black buck antelope nearly died from eating a plastic container, numerous animals suffered broken backs and legs from harassment by dogs, and a cat with its legs taped together was set afire and thrown into a bear pit in an attempt to lure a bear out of its den.[8]

Another concerned citizen, Jan Schaffer, similarly used the Pueblo Chieftain as a forum for making an appeal to the citizens of Pueblo on behalf of the beleaguered inhabitants of the Zoo.

> This is addressed to all those people who want more animals at the City Park Zoo. For the typical zoo goer, it's a nice place to wander, feed the ducks and be entertained. Unfortunately, for other people the entertainment is at the expense of the animals. It is a fact that animals entrusted to our zoo have been harassed, maimed and killed. Ducks have been killed and badly maimed by dogs and kids out for some sick "fun." Have you ever seen the hen mallard whose upper bill is missing? That's the result of some children trying to catch ducks with fishhooks. She survives in spite of it—but many of her kind have not. The bear pits and monkey island have been used as giant trash cans and targets for rock throwers. The hooved animals have been tormented by dogs running the fences. Before we start speaking out for more animals, let's work toward improving the security for those we already have. Those of us who enjoy the zoo and want to improve and preserve it would not object to a small admission charge. The monies taken in would be put back into the zoo. A large fence needs to be erected that would surround the entire zoo; an enclosure that would provide 24-hour

---

[7] Mr. and Mrs V. Vanell, Letter to the Editor, *The Pueblo Chieftain*, July 30, 1978.
[8] "Veterinarian Recalls Cases of Malicious Cruelty," *The Pueblo Chieftain*, May 9, 1978.

protection, with an admittance gate, where fees could be collected. The potential is there. The interest of the general public is there. Now we need to get the city government there. If you want to help your zoo, contact Fred Weisbrod [City Manager] or the city council. We showed them what they could do with Fort Carson, now let's show them what we can do for the zoo![9]

Ms. Schaffer's letter succeeded in capturing the attention of the Zoological Society, which promptly responded pleadingly via the same forum.

> There was mute testament pictured in a recent Public Forum of Jan Schaefer's observation that the Pueblo Zoo's animals are indeed harassed, maimed and/or killed by some members of a thoughtless citizenry. The Zoological Society is indebted to Ms. Schaefer for calling the public's attention once more to this ongoing, very serious problem. This society could use the help of more such caring people. Until this community, including local government, is concerned enough to make the zoo a top priority, indignity and possibly death will be the lot of more of the zoo's permanent residents. We strive, but obviously, only extra funding will provide the full security that is needed at the zoo.[10]

Sometime in 1978, a woman publicly complained about conditions for a leopard that was housed in a small cage in one of the wings of the Animal House. Zoological Society Secretary Margaret Crader responded to the leopard housing complaint in a letter to the editor of *The Pueblo Chieftain*.

> We do care about the inhabitants of the zoo ... and have been working strenuously toward that end for one and a half years. When we did an analysis of the zoo's needs initially, and recognized the scope of what had to be accomplished and no funds to realize it, it was disheartening. Success is not instant. To cite a few of the problems we faced besides no funds, the zoo has no director. Fencing was totally inadequate to protect the animals from daily public harassment. We have since acquired partial extra fencing. We are fully aware of the limitations of the animal house that dates back to WPA days. That will eventually be remedied. We should have education facilities to inform the public and especially the children. To that end we take a wildlife program into the elementary schools. We are limited only by the number of people willing to assume the docent role. The program is very popular, and at present the demands for it exceed our ability to comply. We plan a new drive for volunteers in the fall. Where large capital expenditures are concerned, and where city hall is instrumental in helping us acquire funds, we have to work slowly. City government is well aware of what has to be done to update the zoo and has promised financial aid as soon as new plans and figures are available. ... Meanwhile, we work patiently. We have the general population behind us as we learned from a professional survey we did last year. Eventually, of course, we will acquire a director. When that time comes everything about the zoo will be in sharp focus. All needs will be recognized and presumably acted upon immediately. We would like to establish the fact that the Society conducts monthly meetings at City Park headquarters on third Thursdays at 7:30 p. m. We invite anyone interested in zoo concerns to come, express his views, and help us work things out within the framework of reality.[11]

---

[9] Jan Schaffer, Letter to the Editor, *The Pueblo Chieftain*, February 8, 1979.
[10] Margaret Crader, Secretary, Pueblo Zoological Society, Letter to the Editor, *The Pueblo Chieftain*, February 25, 1979.
[11] Margaret Crader, Secretary, Pueblo Zoological Society, Letter to the Editor, *The Pueblo Chieftain*, June 11, 1978.

The woman who had lodged the initial complaint about the leopard cage subsequently started a fund to make improvements, but after collecting several hundred dollars, the Parks Department discovered that it was a scam. The woman had absconded with the money.

By 1979, the Zoological Society realized that the Zoo needed someone in charge.[12] So alongside pushing for physical improvements, the Society advocated for the hiring of a zoo director. But City officials always had excuses. They claimed that there was not enough money, or that it would be hard to create a civil service position. That did not stop the Society from asking, nor did it endear its members to the existing zookeepers, who were not keen on additional supervision.

The City's annual report on citywide operations in 1979 documents the addition of several new animals at the Zoo: bobcat, zebra, wallabies, emus, and various reptiles. The report also listed several improvements, including additional fencing around the Old Bear Pits and behind the Animal House to prevent vandalism, a new roof on the Animal House, elevated feeders for hoofstock, painting of the Animal House, installation of new paths and a bridge over the moat from the Animal House to the prairie dog town, signs for exhibits, and modification of three cages, including the one for the leopards.

Margaret Crader, by then Zoological Society President, formally asked City Council in 1980 to fence the Zoo and add a 25-cent admission fee. She further requested, since the Park concession stand was being moved out of the Tropical Bird House and into a new facility, that the stone structure of the Bird House be preserved and remodeled to accommodate the zoo education program.[13]

Improvements costing $6,000 that were made during 1980 included the placement of safety railing atop the stone wall around the moat between Happy Time Ranch and the Animal House to prevent children from falling into the water and to prevent dogs from injuring waterfowl plus the installation of a few new windows for the Animal House.

The Pueblo Chieftain printed a long interview with Jonnie and Marti in October 1981 regarding the Zoological Society and noted that the Zoological Society organization already had considerable community and financial support coming from several foundations and organizations. Marti hoped to use the proceeds from a request for $34,700 already submitted to the City for the installation of a path to the hoofstock pens, the completion of the perimeter fencing, and the addition at the Zoo entry of a coin-operated gate that would facilitate the institution of a small admission fee. Marti said, "What we really want to teach is respect for the Zoo. Studies show that people treat something better if they pay for it."[14] Zoological Society goals included making exhibits more attractive for visitors and more comfortable for the animals, the expansion of its animal adoption fund-raising program, and finding companions for solitary animals. Long-range goals included the construction of animal food-prep and veterinary areas, the renovation of outdated facilities, the establishment of a limited breeding program, and the creation of a position for a zoo director.[15]

---

[12] "Zoological Society Seeks Zoo Director," *The Pueblo Chieftain*, March 18, 1979.
[13] "Zoo News: Funds Sought for Face Lift," *The Pueblo Chieftain*, January 23, 1980.
[14] "It's All Happening at the Zoo …," *Pueblo Star Journal and Sunday Chieftain*, October 11, 1981.
[15] "Can Do Zoo Group," *The Pueblo Chieftain*, October 11, 1981.

Meeting the short-term goals of completing fencing around the Zoo and instituting an admission fee would discourage vandalism and possibly provide some funds for other improvements.[16] The lack of proper fencing was a pressing concern since there was otherwise little to protect the animals from being fed inappropriate foods or suffering harassment. With these thoughts in mind, Marti talked to the directors of several other zoos, each of whom felt strongly that establishing a fee had to be a priority. Subsequently, Clayton Freiheit, Denver Zoo Director, was invited to speak at a Zoological Society meeting. He was very gracious, helpful, and informative, and it was extremely valuable to be able to quote his advice to the City Council.[17]

The Zoological Society did a lot of politicking—meeting informally with individual Council members and making a presentation at a Council work session. These efforts were successful, and $34,700 was allocated by the Council to fence the north side of the property in the spring of 1982 and to build a turnstile entrance so that a twenty-five cents per person entry fee could be instituted. The Zoological Society was delighted, even though as many as eight people and a stroller often crammed together into the turnstile, with the whole group entering on a single quarter.

The new front gate, complete with "in" and "out" turnstiles.

(*Image courtesy of the Pueblo Zoological Society*)

[16] The Zoological Society's presentation to City Council in October 1981 listed the following acts of vandalism: 2 swans stoned to death (1975); 2 Canada geese killed (1978); marsh hawk killed, 8 peahens, 12 chickens, and 2 Swainson's hawks stolen (1980); dog on Monkey Island, door of house and window in Happy Time Ranch damaged, 6 decorative wood animals destroyed, bird cage and bridge railing damaged in 1981. Dogs and drunks were a constant problem. A 1976 article in The Pueblo Chieftain revealed that on two occasions blackbuck antelope had required treatment after eating plastic trash thrown into their pen, while a 1977 article described injuries inflicted by two young teens to three ducks and a Canada goose. In 1981, one of the glass doors of the Animal House was broken during the night.

[17] Clayton Freiheit became a long-term friend, always willing to offer advice and encouragement to those of us at a little zoo way down in Southeastern Colorado.

On October 18, 1981, *The Pueblo Chieftain* published an editorial entitled "Can-Do Zoo Group."

> In this era of waning volunteerism, the fine work of the Pueblo Zoological Society is to be greatly admired. It is an encouraging example of how caring citizens can, without massive government assistance, enrich their communities. Using the City Park Zoo as a base of operations, the society has established an impressive program of zoo education. In area schools alone, some 8,000 children have benefitted from outreach sessions and an invaluable field trip to the zoo. Leading the program are Jonnene McFarland and Marti Osborn, both of whom are trained in biology and are part-time employees of the City Parks and Recreation Department. But they couldn't succeed without the assistance of 18 volunteer instructors — "docents" — who share their time and knowledge to help educate the public about animals and the environment. ... and congratulate all 127 members of the zoological society for their contributions to Pueblo and Southeastern Colorado. Also deserving of recognition are the local service organizations and private donors who have given financial support to the society's projects.

In 1981, the Junior League of Pueblo and the Zoological Society, as a part of the City's Discover Pueblo program, made possible twelve directional signs intended to guide visitors to the Zoo.[18] The City had the signs fabricated and installed them along several city streets. But where the Zoological Society had asked the City for the word "zoo" and an arrow, the Public Works staff improved on the idea and included the Zoo's logo. That had the unintended effect of making the signs very attractive to thieves, however, and many were indeed stolen.

Another enterprise during this period was the opening of the Zoovenir Gift Shop. Getting it to the point of making a profit proved to be challenging, however. It began on a simple table in the Animal House lobby before moving into an outdated and unused bus kiosk placed in front of the Animal House by the well-meaning Parks Department. When summer came, the volunteers balked at working inside what was essentially a solar-heated oven. The shop therefore moved next to a small barn that had been built at the entrance to the Happy Time Ranch. That was a little better, but it was still not ideal. When rain leaked through the porous roof and soaked all of the merchandise, the t-shirts were hung up to dry and then sold anyway. And if the wind blew, a layer of sand covered everything.

The shop would move two more times—in 1986 into the new Education Building and again in 1993 where it finally had a space of its own and became profitable in the newly built addition to the Education Building.

Animal Concerns

The Zoological Society was not involved in the acquisition and disposition of animals at the Zoo prior to the 1980s, but the more we learned, the more concerned we became. In 1982, yaks appeared in one of the pens—yes, seemingly just appeared. A reportedly less-than-scrupulous commercial animal dealer brought in the shaggy yearlings, apparently—at least to the Pueblo Zoological Society —without plan or forethought. If ever there was a species poorly

---

[18] "Discover Pueblo to Work with Zoological Gardens," *The Pueblo Chieftain*, June 11, 1980. The "Discover Pueblo" was a City program aimed toward promoting local tourism.

adapted to Pueblo's hot summer climate, yaks were it. After the Society complained about the inappropriateness of the acquisition, the Parks Department transferred them to another facility.

Another episode, this time involving a monkey, gives further evidence that changes were needed. Realizing that a lone male monkey in one of the small cages in the Animal House was not a good thing, the Zoological Society decided to purchase a mate. The new adopt-an-animal program (Animals Depend On People, Too), developed by Shelly Thomas, seemed like the perfect tool for raising the money. Unfortunately, it did not raise enough. So Shelly asked the owners of a local restaurant to help raise the rest. They agreed to have a Sunday morning breakfast in February 1982. Because they provided the food and their staff volunteered, all proceeds from the very successful event went toward obtaining the monkey.

One of the zookeepers made all the arrangements to obtain a female to be shipped to Denver's airport. As a representative of the Society, Marti was invited to ride along with two City employees to pick up the monkey. The two men sat in the front seats of the City's old van, while Marti sat in a folding chair in the back (yes, a folding chair just perched in the back of a van!). Once back at the Zoo with the crated monkey, Marti went home, not having been told about the plan for introducing the animals to each other.

A couple of days later, Marti went to a high school to present an endangered species program to a biology class. At the end of the presentation, one of the students raised his hand and said, "I volunteer at the veterinary clinic, and a monkey from the Zoo was brought in all beaten up and died." Marti was speechless and headed directly to the Parks Director's office. There she was told an attack by the male on the new female, who had suddenly appeared in his territory, resulted in severe injuries. Needless to say, it was an extremely distressing and embarrassing situation for all concerned. Fortunately, the Parks Director found a way to temper the situation, obtaining another female monkey and seeing that it was introduced to the male carefully and properly.

The Zoological Society continued to be concerned about the many problems at the Zoo, as illustrated by both the yak and monkey incidents, and continued to advocate for improvements. The 50-plus year-old "meat house," for example, was not an adequate place for the storage and preparation of animal food, for veterinary care, or for the staff lunchroom, although the zookeepers always kept it clean.[19] Because the Society Board, Marti, and Jonnie all rarely shied away from approaching the "powers-that-be," they tackled the project, making a presentation to City Council during a session at the Parks Department office, after which the two groups toured the Zoo together. The first stop was the "meat house." Not long after the tour the City granted the Parks Department funding for a new building.

The new building, centrally located inside the Zoo, was completed in 1982 and included a kitchen and break-room, a restroom, a storage room for grains and other supplies, a walk-in refrigerator and a freezer, as well as offices for the head zookeeper and the veterinarian.

---

[19] The building had been known since the 1930s by the disturbing name "meat house" because it was used to store raw meat for the feeding of the Zoo's carnivores, prior to the availability of specially manufactured foods specifically intended for exotic animals in zoos.

Although progress was being made, 1982 turned out to be a turbulent year. The Zoological Society was becoming more and more a thorn in the side of the Parks Department. The Society caused the City folks considerable consternation when John Moore, Director of Albuquerque's Rio Grande Zoo, was invited to speak at a public meeting. Marti and Jonnie took him on a tour and to meet Parks Department and City officials. Unfortunately, his talk was a scathing analysis of everything that was wrong with the Zoo and its management. Although this perhaps bolstered the Society's evidence that the facility was badly in need of improvements, it so angered those City and Parks Department officials that it proved to be more a detriment than a help. Once things had calmed down, the Society continued to advocate for both physical and managerial improvements.

A suggestion had emerged as early as 1980 for the construction of a building dedicated solely to housing the Zoological Society's existing education program.[20] Up until that time, the program and its volunteers had operated for several years out of a closet in the Parks Department office. The closet eventually became crammed full of equipment and biofact specmens, and each time it was opened a stuffed armadillo came careening down.

Since it likely would be a long time before a new building answered the education program's need for more space, Marti asked the Parks Department for one of the restrooms in the old Tropical Bird House that had been abandoned when the concession stand moved to a new facility. Marti thought it could be cleaned up with volunteers remodeling the interior. When Parks Department Recreation Director Tony Langoni heard this request, he must have thought we were nuts and took pity on us, offering us part of the fifty-year-old Golf Clubhouse instead. It was a large stone building about two city blocks from the entrance to the Zoo. Another non-profit group occupied the majority of the building, but the Zoological Society was given two rooms that had been added to the north side of the building sometime in the distant past. We were delighted that the Society finally had its own space.

Before we moved in to the new office, we received the Zoological Society's first grant—$1,000 from the Thatcher Foundation for furnishings and an Apple IIE computer. About a year earlier, Jonnie had been hired part-time by the Parks Department, and after receiving this grant, she was warned by the director about mishandling such a large sum of money. He repeated the story about the woman who raised money to build a better leopard exhibit but instead absconded with the funds. Regardless of his good intentions, it was an extremely difficult and upsetting encounter. As a result, both of us felt like giving up, but with the support of many loyal friends in the Zoological Society, we soldiered on, equipping the office and carefully accounting for every last penny.

After moving into our new office and when winter came, we discovered the small wall heater did not add much warmth to the un-insulated addition that jutted out on the north side of the building. Even wearing several layers of clothing, two pairs of heavy socks, and boots, we nearly froze to death. So we bought a kerosene heater. Unfortunately, although we got toasty warm, our heads began to ache. We were being poisoned by carbon monoxide from burning propane in a closed room—a dangerous lesson!

---

[20] "Education Building Funds Being Sought by Zoological Society," *The Pueblo Chieftain*, November 12, 1980.

The Zoological Society office remained in the Golf Clubhouse for a number of years, but as the organization and its programs grew, it was much too small and was inconveniently located outside the entrance to the Zoo itself. So the Zoological Society began lobbying for a new building. Laura Mattoon and the two of us even "crashed" an informal City Council meeting on the subject. Laura was aware that we legally could sit in on the meeting, so the three of us did— more than a little bit uncomfortably. City Council allocated $192,500 for the building to include a large discovery room, animal kitchen, two offices, and a classroom, as well as lobby space for a gift shop and cashier window.

As the education program grew, Jonnie first joined Marti as a part-time employee of the Parks Department, with each working about 20 hours a week. By the mid 1980s, both were working part-time for the Society also, in addition to their Parks Department jobs. But, as had increasingly become the case, neither stayed within the bounds of authority granted by their new part-time Society zoo educator positions. They were bound to get in trouble, and indeed they did. Wearing their Zoological Society hats, they attended City Council meetings to lobby. Then, wearing their City hats, they worked with the Parks Department and an architect to produce plans for the new education building. Unfortunately, when they learned that the plan called for the public to enter the building through an untended door directly into the area that had been proposed as a discovery room, they realized there was a serious problem. Board member Laura Mattoon encountered the architect at a social event and mentioned that Jonnie and Marti had concerns with this part of the design. The following Monday morning, Marti was called into the Parks Department office and given a severe reprimand because the Director felt she and Jonnie had gone behind his back. Marti was so upset that she quit her job on the spot. Later that day, the Parks Director asked her to come back, but she felt it had become too uncomfortable to work for the City. She would instead work only for the Zoological Society. Jonnie took over Marti's City hours. It would turn out to be the best thing that could have happened.

The Mahlon T. White Discovery Room

Developing the Mahlon T. White Discovery Room in the new Education Building was one of the Zoological Society's most effective endeavors and proved to be one of the highlights of all that the two of us accomplished at the Zoo. Had local citizens been surveyed, they likely would not have chosen a discovery room as the Zoo's next new exhibit. Once it was completed, however, visitation spiked to the highest it had been since accurate counts had begun to be taken.

The idea of a discovery room came from David Jenkins, then Curator of Education at the Toledo Zoo, where he recently had opened one. He made an informal presentation about that exhibit at the 1982 International Zoo Educators Association Conference, which the two of us attended in Tucson, Arizona. We immediately thought it was an exciting idea, and so we borrowed David's presentation slides to show to the Zoological Society Board and Parks Department officials. Laura Mattoon was equally excited and showed the slides to Mahlon Thatcher "Butch" White. Almost immediately the Zoological Society received a $40,000 grant from the Thatcher Foundation, and we were off and running!

In addition to the many biological specimens that we had accumulated through the years, we began gathering all sorts of new things to display. Because our personal philosophy was that people in a digital age would be looking for real experiences, we hoped to make the room a hands-on biology book. We brought David Jenkins to Pueblo to help guide initial development of the room's layout and the content of exhibits.

We had plenty of other ideas but needed a lot of help in making them into interesting and educational displays that were still tough enough for a great deal of public use, and all without taking on the cost of hiring an expensive professional exhibit design firm. Local artist Richard Montano answered our call and made the room happen at a cost that fit with our budget.

It took well over a year to finish the exhibits, with much of this work being done while the building was still under construction. We stored the materials for the displays in our small office, crammed between and on top of office furniture, gift shop inventory, and education animals in cages. One needed a map to get through the clutter! The two of us spent long hours researching materials with the help of John King, a recently-graduated biology major. In addition, we had the help of wonderful volunteers, including Art Schwager, Virginia Smith, and Laura Mattoon, who

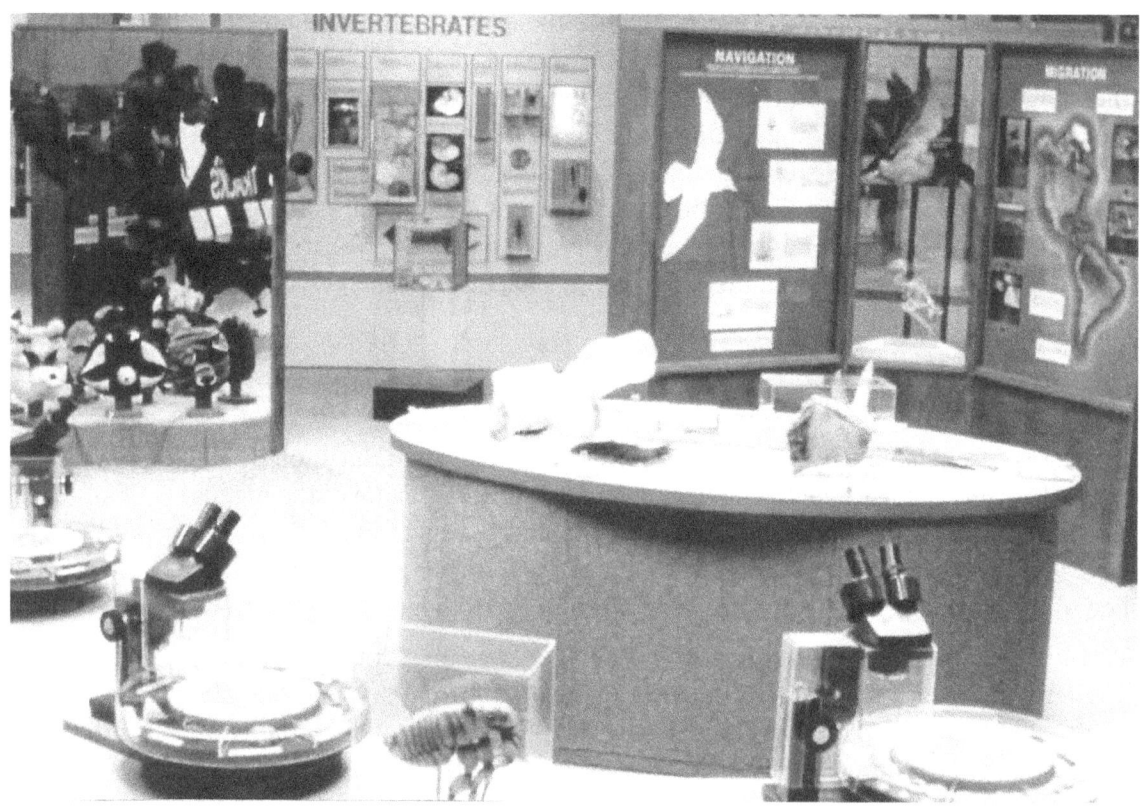

In 1985, the Mahlon T. White Discovery Room was packed with biofact specimens to be explored through magnifiers, under microscopes, or by touching.

(*Image courtesy of the Pueblo Zoological Society*)

all worked tirelessly on the exhibits, helping with the installations right up to an hour before the official opening celebration on June 22, 1985 as the Mahlon T. White Discovery Room, in honor of the Zoological Society's benefactor. It was the first interactive learning center of its kind in Colorado. We are forever grateful to Mahlon "Butch" and Maylan White for allowing us to have this fantastic experience.

In the five months after it opened, there were 22,150 visitors plus nearly two thousand school students. Visitor comments included: "Wish we had something like this at our [Salt Lake City] zoo." "Even better than the Denver Zoo." "The girls had a great time—so did great auntie." It was so very satisfying to watch families learning together—children reading information to their parents and parents helping children understand the items they found on the "What Is It?" table. Children often could be seen "dragging" their parents down the hall to experience the room they previously had explored with a school class.

Jonnie and Marti at the celebration for the opening of the
Education Building and Discovery Room—good food and drinks,
as well as matching animal print shirts for staff and volunteers.

(*Image courtesy of the Pueblo Zoological Society*)

Cold-Blooded Creatures

The next major project undertaken at the Zoo by the City and Zoological Society was what would be called Cold-Blooded Creatures. Reptiles and amphibians fascinated both of us, so we thought the Zoo needed to exhibit a few. We were joined by one of the City zoo keepers. Having previously worked at a reptile garden, he put together a small collection that eventually grew into a wall of aquariums housed at that time in the Animal House. In 1985, the Parks Department applied for and received a $35,000 Community Development Block Grant to rehabilitate the empty Tropical Bird House as a herpetarium for exhibition of reptiles and amphibians. But to do the job right, more money was needed, so the Zoological Society agreed to help by raising $33,000 for the exhibits. Once again, David Jenkins came to Pueblo to help with the design—ten large, glass-fronted exhibits to house animals from rattlesnakes, geckos, and chuckwallas, to bullfrogs and Gila monsters. At the east end of the building, Richard Montano built an open diorama depicting a South American watering hole, complete with live red-legged tortoises, Jonnie's pet iguana, and a simulated termite mound. Always attempting to make use of everything, we had Richard fasten the old stuffed armadillo (its head by then badly damaged by its falls from the closet) into the mound so only its rear end showed, as if it were clawing its way inside to find the tasty termites. Richard also created two life-size sculptures of an anaconda and a Komodo dragon. At the anaconda, a sign asked, "What did the snake eat?" Pushing a button lit up its stomach to reveal a very large pig.

Richard also repaired a gigantic stuffed and mounted Nile crocodile that had been loaned to the Zoo by the US Fish and Wildlife Service. It had been damaged when the authorities had ripped its abdomen open, possibly in search of contraband. Richard patched the creature's belly with fiberglass, rendering the damage invisible. We could only imagine what people thought as he drove from his studio to the Zoo with a giant crocodile strapped on top of his small Toyota pickup.

Richard very literally worked up until the very last minute before the grand opening of the building on August 29, 1986.[21] He continued to work while a committee set up a bar and put out hors d'oeuvres. Guests began to come through the front gate. We dashed to the gift shop, pulled out a colorful t-shirt, hurried to where Richard was applying the last bit of paint to the diorama, asked him to change into the clean shirt, and then brought him out for the ribbon cutting and festivities.

Although busy with both the Education Building and the Cold-Blooded Creatures herpetarium, the Zoological Society continued to be a thorn in the side of the Parks Department. There was a problem with a polar bear. Nobody considered how high these gigantic animals can jump.[22] In the New Bear Pits there was a fairly young, beautiful, energetic, and very strong one. Visitors would hold their children up and over the concrete wall of the exhibit to get a better look. Several Society members saw the bear jump, trying to swipe at children with its massive paw. We showed a

---

[21] Unfortunately, the planned opening was delayed several weeks, when late in 1985 vandals broke twelve brand new double paned, 5' x 5' windows in the building, doing an estimated $10,000 in damage. See "Vandalism Zoo Toll is $10,000," *The Pueblo Chieftain*, February 20, 1986.

[22] Evidently a swimming polar bear is able to jump about 8 feet out of the water when grabbing a seal. Jen Green, *Bears: Amazing Animal Hunters* (Mankato, MN: Amicus, 2011).

To make the Komodo dragon, Richard drilled each scale individually into the fiberglass model.
(*Image courtesy of the Pueblo Zoological Society*)

Nile crocodile suspended in the Cold-Blooded Creatures building.
(*Image courtesy of the Pueblo Zoological Society*)

photograph of this behavior to the Parks Department Director, and it was not long until the bear was sent to another zoo.

One thing that particularly bothered the Parks Department management was the Zoological Society's idea to build a better, healthier exhibit for one of the public's favorites, Solar Sue, the sun bear. The section of the New Bear Pits that she occupied had a concrete floor that greatly irritated her feet as she paced back and forth in the confined area. Although the veterinarian tried to treat them, her feet continued to crack, bleed, and form open sores. The Society raised $3,000 to install an oval, welded wire cage similar to the ones that housed the birds of prey.[23] To be located under shade trees, the cage would have a dirt floor and a heated den, thus providing a more natural habitat for the small, tropical bear. Because installation of the cage required a sewer connection and foundation, which Society funds would not cover, the Parks Department spent a considerable amount of their annual capital budget on the project. Sue moved into her new home in 1986 and lived there for many years. Despite getting grief from the City, the only thing that mattered to the Society was that Solar Sue's feet healed.

It was becoming obvious to both the City and the Zoological Society by 1986 that an official plan was needed to guide growth and change—hopefully, to get everyone headed in the same direction. Having met David Jenkins during development of the Discovery Room and the Cold-Blooded Creatures exhibits, the Parks Director hired him to complete a master plan for the Zoo. David brought along Gary Lee and Jon Coe, who would go on to become two of the foremost zoo designers in the world. The City paid David, Jon, and Gary a total of $5,000— certainly a very meager amount by their subsequent standards. Considering Pueblo's extremes in weather and its financial constraints, they suggested that the Zoo display only native species. Unfortunately, when the plan was publicized, the public made it clear they did not like that idea, thinking "native" meant only rattlesnakes and tarantulas! There was a very vocal fuss in the media. Consequently, although much of this plan became the foundation for future ones, in order to satisfy its constituents the Zoo continued to focus on animals from around the globe.

Since its founding ten years earlier, the Zoological Society had been asking for perimeter fencing and had seen one installed along the north side of the property. In 1987, someone tossed two dingo-like dogs over into the south-side pen of Wentworth, the Zoo's first, and at that time only, red kangaroo. The dogs chased the animal until it hit a fence and broke its neck. That was a truly sad day for the two of us. It was painful to walk into the veterinary area to find such a wonderful animal stretched out on a table, dead. Of course, we also were very angry and headed directly to the Parks Department Director's office. To his credit, he understood our concerns and worked to secure funds to build a fence on the south side along Nuckolls Avenue. By 1988, the Zoo was completely fenced, although the west side was not secure from October through March, when the ditch that runs along that side was empty.

The United States Department of Agriculture (USDA) the licensing body for animal exhibitors, had cited the City for conditions in both bear pits. One citation led to the Old Bear Pits being

---

[23] These cages were modified corncribs manufactured by Behlen, the company whose products were for many years the primary form of corn storage in the U.S.

emptied in 1986 with the removal of the last two animals, a Kodiak bear and a Grizzly bear. The second citation recommended that no more than two species be exhibited in the New Bear Pits because wastewater flowed from one animal area to the next before reaching a single drain, making it impossible to prevent the spread of disease from one pit to the next. With concerns about zookeeper and visitor safety and only two species permitted, the New Bear Pits had become an unacceptable exhibit structure, and the few remaining animals were moved elsewhere. The Parks Department and the Zoological Society agreed that, instead of demolishing them, the pits would be used as the foundation of a new exhibit building. Gary Lee came again to Pueblo to develop concepts for new exhibits to be installed inside the new building.[24] He suggested it be called the Ecocenter. In 1987, the Society launched a capital campaign to raise $250,000 to match the City's allocation, which was for roofing, renovation of the building, and addition of utilities. In 1989, the City began construction, and in 1990 the Society agreed to work with them on completing the interior and installing animal exhibits. There would be many changes to the Zoological Society and the Zoo, however, before this major project could be completed.

The new concrete block walls of the Ecocenter being built in 1990.

(*Image courtesy of the Pueblo Zoological Society*)

---

[24] In the future we would meet with Gary Lee by traveling to either the Cheyenne Mountain Zoo in Colorado Springs or to the Denver Zoo, both places where his firm did much exhibit design work. At these times, his design advice was offered pro bono.

The Last Straw

In February 1989, while we both were attending the second year of the American Association of Zoological Parks and Aquariums Management School in Morgantown, West Virginia, we received word that on a bitterly cold night a newborn waterbuck had frozen to death. Additionally, within a couple of weeks, it became obvious that a pair of dama gazelles had suffered frost bitten hooves. Within months, their legs became infected, and they, too, were dead. The Zoological Society was furious that the Parks Department had accepted such delicate species for the Zoo but had not provided adequate winter quarters for them. Consequently, the group decided to build a heated barn.

Local philanthropists Bob and Doris Johnston came to the Zoological Society's aid by sponsoring a barbeque to raise funds to purchase materials, to secure pledges for additional monies, and to enlist the in-kind services of builders. Bob believed that a few strong drinks prompted folks to open their wallets, and so the invitation read, "Those of you who are unable to break into a barn raising frame of mind without assistance may partake in our therapy at the bar and maintain your health by eating BBQ, beans, and salad."

After enlisting volunteer architect John Hurtig to design the barn and volunteer contractor Charlie Rumsey to oversee construction, Bob twisted the arm of a bricklayer to lay the over-sized block walls and then rolled up his sleeves to work right along with him. Dubbed the Savannah Barn in future years, it was a substantial building, with rebar and concrete stabilized exterior walls, brick stall walls, floors sloped to the drains (one of the most critical issues in zoo construction), and an old-fashioned but very efficient cupola for ventilation.

About the same time, the Parks Director hired a Denver Zoo curator to advise him on the operation of the Zoo. This animal husbandry specialist expressed his concerns about construction of the barn, saying that if the zookeepers put animals into it, they would be unmanageable, likely killing themselves. The zookeepers, who did not want to bother with a barn in the first place, then were convinced that nobody in the Zoological Society knew what they were doing and refused to use the new structure.

The barn became the proverbial "straw that broke the camel's back." The Zoological Society and the two of us were working very hard to make things better at the Zoo, but somehow things were becoming more and more frustrating. It was becoming clear that there had to be a change, perhaps a drastic change. In an editorial published in July of 1989, *The Pueblo Chieftain* questioned the Zoo's future.

> Slowly but surely, the Pueblo Zoo has become a worthy object of community pride. Through the cooperative efforts of the Pueblo Zoological Society's volunteers and the City Parks and Recreation Department, the zoo has been transformed from a backwater operation to one that handsomely displays a significant variety of animals. A trip to the zoo can be an entertaining and educational experience, particularly for families with children. Now the Zoological Society is asking the city for guidance. At issue is how extensive should the zoo

Savannah Barn just after completion.

(*Image courtesy of the Pueblo Zoological Society*)

become. Pueblo probably can't afford to build one on the scale of Cheyenne Mountain Zoo. On the other hand, young families can afford the Pueblo Zoo's modest entrance fees. Some even come from Colorado Springs to patronize it. We believe it should be kept affordable for the people who utilize it the most. The city administration is sympathetic to the Zoological Society's request but would rather delay long-range planning until it can hire a qualified director, possibly next year. While that approach is understandable, there are some steps that should be undertaken in the meantime. The city should conduct market research to determine what kinds of displays the zoo's patrons would like to see and how much more they would be willing to pay for the privilege. Having that information would provide a rational basis for planning. Whatever additions are made will not come cheap. The city's current cost of operating the zoo is about $260,000. Last year the city recouped $26,200 through admission charges and anticipates similar income this year. Despite all the other tugs on the municipal budget, we believe it is in the community's best interest to continue improving the zoo. It is a valuable community asset, one which makes Pueblo a more attractive place to live for life-long citizens and newcomers alike. It's an investment in our community, both for the present and the future.[25]

[25] "A Community Asset," *The Pueblo Chieftain*, July 14, 1989.

Although conditions for the Zoo's animals were improving, tensions continued to increase between the Zoological Society—a group that did not feel it had enough input or control—and the Parks Department, which seemed to feel the Society was getting more and more out of control. Now was time to make a sweeping change or give up. The years 1989 and 1990 would prove to be pivotal, with the two of us and the Society forging forward without the lengthy feasibility studies and plans generally called for in forming private-public partnerships.

"We are at a crossroads," Marti told the newspaper. "We need to move forward, or we're just going to die." Working with Councilman Bud Whitlock, the Zoological Society proposed that they assume management of the facility. Whitlock commented that privatization would cost the City the same amount, while resulting in a "better Zoo." Parks Director Tony Langoni stated that he did not mind the Society taking the Zoo from his department, "It's fine with me as long as they run it fence to fence."[26] City Manager Lew Quigley was quoted as saying that work was progressing to determine the cost of a contract and how to absorb seven Zoo employees (four zookeepers, two part-time cashiers, plus Jonnie) into City operations. According to Marti, the Society would employ a director and a curator, and then establish long-term goals.[27]

The Pueblo Chieftain followed with a very supportive editorial.

> The City and the Pueblo Zoological Society are negotiating an agreement to privatize the operations of the Pueblo Zoo. Under the proposal, the Society would hold a three-year contract to manage the zoo. Zoo workers would be employed by the Society, which also would hire a specially trained animal curator. It's not a new concept. Numerous communities have contracted for management of their zoo operations. Atlanta, for example, has reported great success in improving its zoo in this manner. Having the zoo administration in private hands would allow greater flexibility in animal acquisitions and long-range planning. At the same time, the zoo would remain under the city's ownership. Puebloans have witnessed how taking a public amenity out of government administration has been beneficial. The Colorado State Fair, once run as an arm of state government, has been able to operate more efficiently and aggressively since its operations were turned over to the State Fair Authority. The Zoological Society has similarly ambitious plans for the zoo. It would like to create better display areas for animals such as bears and large cats. The Society has a proven track record in its ability to get things done. Largely through its efforts and guidance, the zoo has been transformed from a nearly forgotten backwater to a center of municipal pride and a real educational asset. We are encouraged that it has proposed to take on this next logical step. City Council should give the Society a go at the job.[28]

By the end of August, there still was no agreement between the Zoological Society and the City. $316,059 was budgeted for operation of the facility in 1991, but the Society was asking for $424,427, which included $25,000 in admission fees to be kept by the Society. Two councilmen were concerned with what appeared to be an increase in funding, while three others—Mike Occhiato, Fay Kastelic, and Bud Whitlock—were supportive. "I think we have a crummy Zoo out

---

[26] We would learn the true meaning of this statement in months to come.
[27] "Privatization of Zoo Proposed to Council," *The Pueblo Chieftain*, July 17, 1990.
[28] "Making a Better Zoo," *The Pueblo Chieftain*, July 20, 1990.

there," Whitlock said. "We don't have a lion, we don't have any bears, and I feel like we have to do something to get the Zoo going."[29]

On October 22, City Council held a critical vote on the proposal. "The Pueblo Zoological Society just may get its chance to make the Pueblo Zoo a roaring success."[30] Working with Marti on developing a contract with the City was Zoological Society President Cathy Spangler and attorney Todd Kettelkamp, who assisted in negotiations pro bono. Even on the eve of the final vote, the City had not finalized the amount of money they would allocate for operation in the following year.[31]

That evening Council voted 5 to 2 to allow the Zoological Society to assume management of the Zoo under a 3-year contract. "We will go along with the contract, but we are not going to give them another penny to run the Zoo," said Councilman Ken Hunter at the meeting. So the City initially decided on the same amount that it had allocated for the Zoo in 1990—$306,059. The final allocation would be $332,059, which included a projected $26,000 in gate fees.[32]

The management transition period was especially stressful for Jonnie. Before the difficulties in 1985 over placement of the discovery room, Marti and Jonnie had each worked half-time for the Parks Department and half time for the Zoological Society. After Marti quit the Parks Department, she worked as the Society's Executive Director. Jonnie became the City's Zoo Educator. But because Jonnie worked directly for the City, she could not play a visible role in the Society's negotiations. She worked quietly behind-the-scenes, particularly in the financial area, and attended many of the Society's strategy meetings. She was ultimately offered the position of Executive Director once the contract between the Society and the City was signed. Marti, meanwhile, moved to the position of Associate Director/Education for the Society. Both were a good fit. Jonnie had both an MBS in Ecology and an MBA as well as financial experience. Marti held a master's degree in biology, a teaching license, and classroom teaching experience.

And so as 1990 was drawing to a close, we moved on to the next and undoubtedly the most challenging phase of our involvement with the Pueblo Zoo. The agreement giving the Zoological Society the authority to manage the 25-acre facility was signed in late October. The Society immediately established a Board committee to interview and hire the first five zookeepers, two cashiers, and a maintenance worker. Advertising and interviews began so a curator could be brought on board as early as possible in the new year.

---

[29] "No Lions, No Bears, No Agreement on Zoo Issue," *The Pueblo Chieftain*, August 22, 1990.
[30] "New Zoo Administration Just Council Vote Away," *The Pueblo Chieftain*, October 22, 1990.
[31] "New Zoo Administration Just Council Vote Away," *The Pueblo Chieftain*, October 22, 1990.
[32] "City OKs Privately Run Zoo," *The Pueblo Chieftain*, October 23, 1990; "Council Stands Behind Pledge for Pueblo's Zoo," *The Pueblo Chieftain*, October 24, 1990.

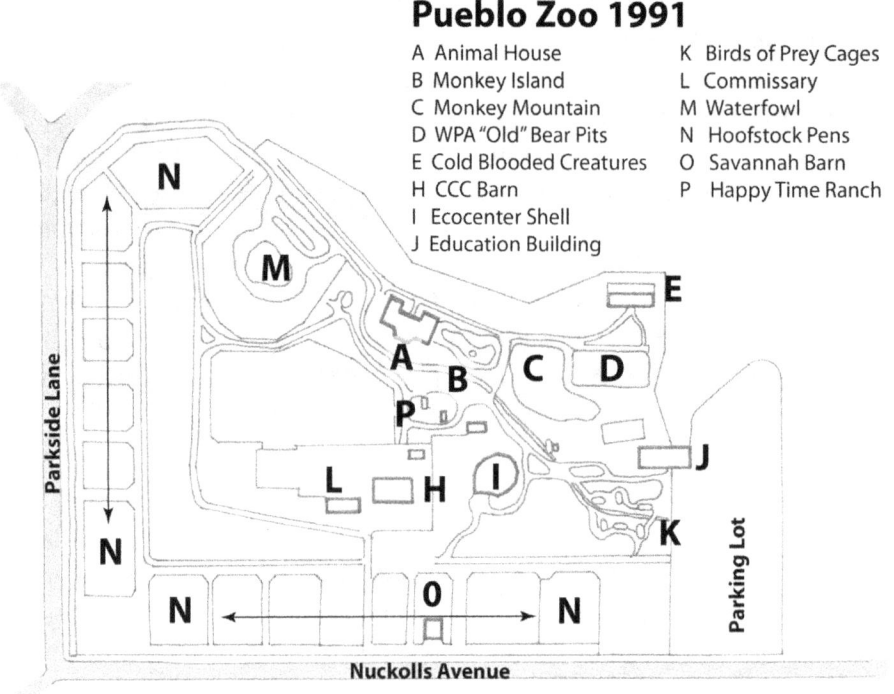

Map of the Pueblo Zoo layout as it appeared in 1991.
(*Drawing by Richard Montano drawing, legend by Steven McDonald*)

Chapter Three

From Fence to Fence:
January 1991 to July 2012

On January 1, 1991, the Pueblo Zoological Society began managing the 25-acre Pueblo Zoo, in the prophetic words of Parks Department Director Tony Langoni, "from fence to fence." Thus began a long chapter in the life of the Society and our tenure there. Over the twenty-one years that this chapter documents, the staff would grow and change, the animal collection would increase from 84 to 138 species, new buildings and exhibits would be built, and all of us would learn so very much about running a zoo.

The Zoological Society's Board of Directors had chosen Jonnie as the their executive director and the Zoo's first director. Marti assumed the position of Associate Director/Education. Five new zookeepers came on board to be trained for the last week of December by the City staff, who were themselves being transferred to other positions and were much less than happy. These five young folks had a rough week. The City's part-time cashiers, a part-time farm keeper, and a part-time maintenance worker remained onboard. Dr. Regis Opferman, despite having expressed a desire to move on, continued as contract veterinarian until Dr. Norman Armentrout assumed the part-time position.

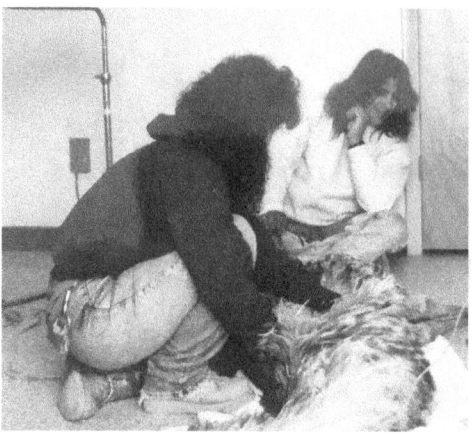

Two of the Zoological Society's five original zookeepers,
Rose Ellen Filangi and Bill Trujillo, check an ailing emu.

(*Image courtesy of the McBirney Family*)

We begin with the mission statement adopted early in 1991. Through the years, the wording would evolve and change, but this version generally expresses what the Zoological Society set out to accomplish.

> ***The Pueblo Zoo seeks to make an impact on present and future generations***
> ***by exhibiting and interpreting varied aspects of the living world***
> ***in an enjoyable setting,***
> ***by participating in the conservation of animal species,***
> ***and by encouraging related research.***

Feeling confident that they could raise private funds to supplement the Zoo's budget, the Zoological Society Board agreed to manage the Zoo with the same amount of money that the City Council had allocated for the previous year. One must wonder how they thought they could do it on such a small budget. Although Jonnie and an accountant poured through the City's records, the actual cost to run the place was difficult to determine. For the first year, we would operate "by the seat of our pants," with no idea whether or not the Society could survive. For instance, very early on, a car careened into the south perimeter fence, and as we paid the bills for an unanticipated major repair, we learned the hard meaning of Tony's remark, "...from fence to fence."

On a very cold New Year's Day our tiny staff, a hard-working board, a handful of volunteers, and the two of us gathered in the Education Building for a chili lunch and then set out to meet the many challenges that the future would bring. But, before describing the challenges of caring for animals and the critical need to improve the Zoo's physical facilities, our story focuses on some of the Zoological Society's less visible challenges. There were many things for which neither our biology nor business degrees prepared us.

Of critical importance was understanding the copious rules and regulations that govern the operation of a zoo—USDA standards for animal care and safety, OSHA rules and Workers' Compensation guidelines for employee safety, insurance company requirements for visitor and building safety, Health Department regulations for food safety, and AZA specifications for everything else. Emergency drills on animal escapes or attacks, grounds evacuation, and severe weather were conducted routinely. Over the next few years we would hire Safety Officer Mary Tucey to coordinate all things related to safety, keeping records of animal care, animal enrichment, and employee matters, as well as extensive calendars of maintenance needs and reporting deadlines. These databases would be developed by Jeanne McFarland-McDonald, who created a similar system for tracking donations and memberships.

Envisioning the future requires both master and strategic planning. During our tenure, we were involved in a number of master plans. David Jenkins, Jon Coe, and Gary Lee completed the first in 1986, followed by ones done by Richard Montano and Gary Lee, University of Southern Colorado facilities designer Phyllis Meckley, and Zoological Society Board member John Ercul. Subsequently, there were many versions of a strategic plan, developed generally under the supervision of docent, donor, and board member Linda Stefanic. For smaller improvement goals, senior staff developed lists of projects to complete each year. Most were financed through a Special Projects Fund that included all profits from animal sales, unrestricted bequests, designated City and County allocations, and restricted grants. The amount spent on special projects each year varied greatly, depending on how much funding was received.[1]

Three major and immediate needs were to combine two telephone systems into one covering twenty-five acres and five widely separated buildings, to establish computer networks, and to determine how to best use hand-held radios for safety. The radios were a particular puzzle. The Zoo's radios were on the powerful City system that required adherence to strict Federal Communications Commission regulations. At first, we shared a channel with the bus system and the airport ground maintenance crew. Although the airport folks did not talk much unless they were mowing or plowing snow, the bus drivers had to report in every half hour, interrupting Zoo conversations, which could have been perilous in an emergency. It took considerable negotiation over a couple of years to be granted a dedicated channel.

Of course, the most visible aspect of the Zoological Society's management of the Zoo was making improvements to the physical facilities. The community's generous response to several capital campaigns together with foundation grants and corporate in-kind contributions resulted in approximately $7,000,000 in capital improvements between 1991 and 2012.

The State of the Zoo at the Beginning of 1991

Education Building: one classroom, two offices, Mahlon T. White Discovery Room, animal kitchen, public restrooms, a small gift shop, and overlooking the Zoo entrance, a cashier window where the newly increased 50-cent admission fee was collected.

---

[1] After coming under Zoological Society management, the Zoo's finances were administered by Finance Manager Tammy Guarienti, as well as by bookkeepers Betty Kolesarek and Julie Jaime.

Education Building in 1991.

(*Image courtesy of the Pueblo Zoological Society*)

Commissary and Adjacent Areas: Food storage, curator office, veterinary office and examination room, restroom, employee lunchroom. Behind this building there was a row of cages built by the WPA in the late 1930s, a run-down building filled with all manner of junk, one chain link cage, a small garage also filled with mostly unusable junk, and a series of runs and stalls.

Animal House: About half of the cages were empty. The only big cats were two snow leopards.

Cold-Blooded Creatures Building: Renovated by the City in 1986, the building featured reptile exhibits installed by the Zoological Society.

Old Bear Pits: Empty since 1989.

New Bear Pits: During 1989 and 1990, the City and Zoological Society worked together to change this circular pit into the Ecocenter. The shell and installation of utilities had been completed, but work ceased in the fall of 1990.

Bird Cages: Dating from the 1960s, five welded wire cages with metal roofs contained a golden eagle, an Andean condor, and several species of pheasants, but there was absolutely no landscaping in the area.

Solar Sue's Cage: This was another welded wire cage, installed by the City and Zoological Society to give the sun bear an acceptable home.

Happy Time Ranch: Several peacocks and many, many goats were allowed to roam freely, damaging buildings and harassing visitors.

Hoofstock Pens: Bison, elk, common eland, beisa oryx, blackbuck, Grant's zebra, and fallow deer (white, spotted, and black). Except for two pens surrounding the new Savannah Barn, all of the pens had open-fronted concrete shelters, some of which had electrical heat.

Other than desks, appliances, and a table in the Commissary, the equipment left by the City for the Zoological Society's use amounted to a couple of antiquated trucks, an unusable van, an ancient AMC Gremlin auto that had been acquired by a City zookeeper in trade for a pair of elk antlers, a golf cart with no wheels, trash cans and a broom, but no rakes. Outbuildings were filled with junk, there was no workshop, there was no garage. Half of the animal exhibits were empty.

During the last week of December 1990 it was bitterly cold, and the thermostat in the Commissary was left very low. As a result, the water pipes running through the ceiling froze and broke, causing the ceiling to collapse, which damaged much of the interior and furnishings. The City ultimately repaired the building, but in the meantime the entire new Zoological Society staff had to work out of the classroom in the Education Building. Much to our dismay, it was impossible to save most of the few existing animal records—soaked inside a file drawer—or the veterinarian's microscope, which was submerged in water inside its wooden box. Furnishings, appliances, and some other equipment were also destroyed.

On the fourth day of Zoo management—on the very cold afternoon of January 4—a common eland gave birth.[2] Nighttime temperatures were predicted to be in the low 20s, which did not seem to us to be favorable for survival of the calf in a door-less, unheated shelter. Of course, the two of us admittedly knew absolutely nothing about caring for large hooved animals, but because an oryx calf had died on a frigid night a couple of years earlier, we did not want to take any chances. It was late in the day, and our only help was Bob Morris, our one-man maintenance crew. He brought one of the trucks, and the three of us entered the pen. Having worked on a ranch, Bob had a pretty good idea what to do, but the two of us were scared to death of the two huge adult animals with their long, sharp horns. Bob managed to isolate the adult male with the truck, and we somehow herded the female and her newborn calf into the previously unused but heated barn. All ended well, the young animal thrived, and we survived![3]

Also within the first week, trash reared its ugly head. For a long, long time, the City zookeepers hauled the daily truckload of manure from the pens to the high south bank of the Arkansas River, where it was dumped. Mysteriously, right at the beginning of January, the City-County Health

---

[2] Common elands are large African antelope with spiral horns that may reach two feet in length. Males weigh in at over a ton, with females up to 1,300 pounds.
[3] Within a few years the barn would become night quarters for zebras, ostriches, crowned cranes, and dik dik.

Jasper, the male eland born on January 4, 1991, and his mother (*left*) were the first animals to use the Savannah Barn.

(*Image courtesy of the Pueblo Zoological Society*)

Department learned of this activity and immediately banned the Zoological Society's zookeepers from dumping there. Of course, it should never have been dumped there in the first place. The next day, KOAA-TV News was in the driveway of Jonnie's home asking how the Society planned to handle the situation. She had no idea. We had no plan! As we would find many times in the future, the community came to our rescue. The man who ran the City landfill under a contract with the City waived all fees for dumping the manure. Although it involved an expensive 30-mile round-trip in an old truck, the Society's zookeepers did it every day without complaint.

Before the first month ended, the US Department of Agriculture inspector arrived to make an unannounced tour of the Zoo because management had changed hands. The inspector cited the facility for several items that were out of compliance with federal regulations. If the necessary improvements were not completed within 60 days, losing the Zoological Society's license to operate the Zoo was a real possibility. What we had not been told was that the Zoo had been documented as out-of-compliance in 1990, and the City had not made or budgeted for the required upgrades. Once again, the community saved us. Philanthropist Bob Johnston and his right-hand man, Ramon Mejia, spent many days using donated materials to make most of the required repairs before the deadline.

The challenges kept coming, and we kept learning the hard way! In early February, a male zebra became suddenly ill. The Zoo's veterinarian, Dr. Regis Opferman, was out of town, so Jonnie called every veterinarian in the area, learning that all those who treated large animals were out vaccinating cattle. Only small-animal veterinarians remained, and one of them, Dr. Bill Krause, responded to the plea for help. He said the problem likely was colic but unfortunately was unable to do much to help the suffering animal. One of Jonnie's next calls was to Cheyenne Mountain Zoo Director Susan Engfer. She recommended a veterinarian who worked there when their regular one was away. Thankfully, Dr. Norman Armentrout was able to head to Pueblo, arriving around 10 PM. He did as much as he could for the zebra, whose condition by that time had deteriorated. As the night wore on, zookeeper Bill Trujillo sat on a bale of straw, cradling the dying animal's head and comforting it until it took its last breath. The cause was a problem with the hay that had been in the barn when the Zoological Society assumed management. We had made the mistake of assuming the hay left in the barn was good enough for horses.

After a national search, Marilyn McBirney came on board as General Curator in February 1991. She brought many years of animal care experience, a vast knowledge of animal behavior, and a boundless enthusiasm for everything about zoos and animals. At last we had the guidance we would need in future hay purchases, as well as in record keeping, exhibit design, and species acquisition.

Accreditation Achieved!

Meanwhile, the Zoological Society had to accomplish its most important goal, which was for the Zoo to be accredited by American Association of Zoological Parks and Aquariums (AAZPA). Had accreditation not been achieved, the City likely would have ended its contract with the Society. The extensive application process began in 1991. Susan Engfer, Director of Cheyenne Mountain Zoo, was very helpful, touring the Zoo and mentoring us through much of the process. Accreditation has high standards not only in animal care and physical facilities, but also in all other aspects of operation, including aesthetics, education and interpretation, conservation, planning, marketing, ethics, governance, safety and security, finance and record keeping, and guest services. At the beginning of 1992, we submitted the lengthy application and identified the physical improvements needed to bring facilities up to accreditation standards. In addition, records had to be developed for 258 individual animals.[4]

In June 1992, after the Zoo's application materials had been accepted, a director, a veterinarian, and a curator from three accredited zoos conducted a two-day inspection. They identified several deficiencies that had to be corrected before the Accreditation Commission met at the AAZPA Annual Meeting in Toronto. Together with General Curator Marilyn McBirney, we appeared before the 16-member commission—certainly a daunting prospect. After the meeting, we could hardly wait to send a press release announcing that the Pueblo Zoo had achieved its first accreditation in September 1992.[5]

---

[4] Some of the animal records were maintained in paper files, others digitally. In the early 1990s, the Zoo became a member of the International Species Inventory System (now Species360), which required some information to be shared with other zoos via programs at that time called Arks and MedArks. It would take years for all of the Zoo's animal records to be kept within one digital system.

[5] Accreditation is not renewed. Because standards are always being raised, zoos must keep up with changes and go through the entire process every 5 years. Under our supervision, the Zoo would go on to accomplish three-and-a-half more. Because the required paperwork multiplied each time, the second (1997), third (2002), and fourth (2007) were not easy, but we knew more about the process by then. The last one, in 2012, we took only as far as the submission of written materials and the on-site inspection.

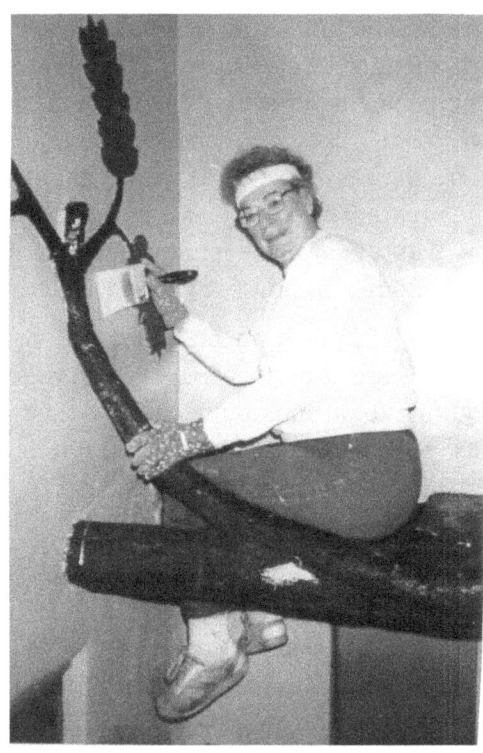

Everyone—staff, board, and volunteers—pitched in to get the Zoo in tiptop shape. Volunteer Betty Wilkinson is shown painting the Animal House cages.

(*Image courtesy of the Pueblo Zoological Society*)

Improving the Zoo Begins

That same year, the Zoo's small staff, together with several volunteers, somehow found the stamina to finish the Ecocenter. The City had completed the shell of the building by mid-1990. Exhibits had to fit within the unusual shape of the concrete walls of what had been the New Bear Pits and which had become the foundation of the new building. Zoo designer Gary Lee's initial concept included three large ecosystem exhibits: a tropical rainforest, a desert, and penguins on an arid shore. We soon eliminated the desert and changed the rainforest into a walk-through exhibit. The first floor included these two exhibit areas and a small animal diet preparation kitchen. Addition of a partial the second story allowed an employee break room, curator office, and penguin isolation area complete with a small pool.

Naturally, no one in Pueblo had any idea how to build a penguin habitat. Having recently visited the Steinhart Aquarium's excellent African black-footed penguin exhibit in San Francisco, Marti suggested we send Richard Montano there to learn how to turn the huge fiberglass pool proposed by the architects into a successful penguin exhibit. Being both an artist and an engineer, Richard returned with photographs, detailed measurements, and a complete understanding of what was

Looking down from a second story window overlooking the exhibit, the photograph shows penguin burrow entrances that lead to nesting boxes with rear access doors for checking eggs or chicks.

(*Image courtesy of John Alderton*)

needed. While the pool, huge window for underwater viewing of the penguins, and a filtration system were being installed, Richard built sections of simulated rocks in his studio by spraying concrete into rubber molds.[6] At the Zoo, he assembled the approximately 4-foot square pieces into a rock wall containing fifteen nest boxes—five in each of three tiers.

Testing the penguin pool revealed an unexpected complication. The pool held water, but when it was drained into what everyone assumed was the sewer, thousands of gallons of water flooded into the service area behind the exhibit. What we did not know was that, between the first phase overseen by the Parks Department and the second phase under Zoological Society control, the sewer line had not been connected to the main.[7] For months all of the wastewater had been oozing out into the dirt around the foundation. To make the critical connection, a very large section of the concrete floor in the service area was removed and replaced at a great, unexpected cost.

As the exhibit was nearing completion, the Zoological Society hired a zookeeper with penguin care experience and introduced ten African black-footed penguins acquired from the Denver Zoo and the Steinhart and Baltimore Aquariums. We were concerned that the penguins would never

---

[6] Within a short time, the contractor went out of business, leaving the Zoo with no warranty. The pool would hold up well for many years, but in the future, the viewing window would give us plenty of grief.

[7] The project was delayed between late 1989 and mid-1991, while management negotiations were underway.

The rainforest, shown here a few years after its initial opening, includes a boa constrictor display inside a huge fallen log.

(*Image courtesy of the Pueblo Zoological Society*)

use the nest boxes on the highest tier, but when they readily moved into all three levels, we realized that Richard had an innate understanding of animal behavior. The exhibit was successful beyond anyone's wildest dreams, its inhabitants producing more than 50 chicks before we retired twenty years later.

Meanwhile, the rainforest was being created. Horticulturist Karen Adams worked with Marti to research and order plant species. Richard sculpted several huge buttressed trees of fiberglass and built a waterfall that flowed into a pond. Eleven species of tropical birds, lesser slow lorises, Geoffrey's tamarins, acouchis, a boa constrictor, and piranhas were introduced into the exhibit, but the poison dart frogs did not arrive in time. Plastic versions had to stand in during the first few days the exhibit was open. (Yes, we cheated!)

While staff hounded contractors, placed plants in the rainforest, hung signs, and introduced animals, a Board committee planned a grand opening for which many of them would don tuxedos (Aren't they called penguin suits?). The opening of the building was celebrated on June 13, 1992 with a big party, held just 18 months after the Zoological Society assumed management of the Zoo.

To recognize donors to the Ecocenter, their names were listed on metal relief sculptures that represented all seventeen of the world's penguin species. Richard Montano created the display that was hung facing the penguin underwater viewing window.

Cutting the Ecocenter ribbon are (left to right) Marti, Board President Corinne Koehler, a young lady representing "The Pennies for Penguins" fund drive, unknown, Mahlon "Butch" White, and City Councilwoman Fay Kastelic.

(*Image courtesy of the McBirney Family*)

Once the Ecocenter was open, the Zoological Society moved on, announcing a $700,000 capital campaign to fund expansion of the Education Building and to build an African lion exhibit. Opened in spring 1993, the 2,200 square foot addition to the education building included a large classroom, public restrooms, a real gift shop, and a ticketing booth.

High on the Zoological Society's list of improvements was replacement of the indoor and outdoor cages that were added to the Animal House in the 1960s. Although they gave the big cats more space and access to fresh air and sunshine, they had an animals-in-jail look. A lioness known as Bo was accepted under the condition she would become the "poster girl" for the capital campaign.

Planning a lion exhibit brought new challenges and lessons—floors had to slope to drains, frequent air exchanges were needed to control strong feline odors, holding cages had to be configured for both zookeeper and animal safety, and the fencing around the outdoor enclosure needed to assure there would be no chance for a big cat escape. Ground was broken on June 9, 1993. Designed by HGF Architects, the exhibit was built by BAV Construction. Richard Montano created a simulated kopje (a tall rock outcropping found in Africa) in the exhibit yard and built a simulated African hut viewing area, where a large bulletproof glass window was installed to give visitors an unimpeded view into the exhibit. Because the environments of animals and humans

The addition to the Education Building, as it appeared in 2003.
Richard Montano made the metal cutout of the Zoo's logo for the tower.

(*Image courtesy of the Pueblo Zoological Society*)

Lion exhibit viewing shelter.

(*Image courtesy of the Pueblo Zoological Society*)

The names of donors to the capital campaign to fund expansion of the Education Building and construction of the African Lion exhibit were stamped onto the copper Mane of Names mounted on the exterior of the south end of the Education Building.

(*Image courtesy of the Pueblo Zoological Society*)

are so intricately interwoven, as with other new exhibits we included cultural as well as animal information in the interpretive graphics installed in the hut. The $326,000 exhibit was officially opened on April 9, 1995, with a celebratory brunch enjoyed by donors and dignitaries. The African-themed landscape won Colorado Lottery Starburst recognition and an award from Association of Zoos and Aquariums Project Habitat.

In July 1993, the *Woman's Focus* interviewed the two of us and General Curator Marilyn McBirney, who by then had become a vital part of the Zoo management team.

> The Pueblo Zoo is run by women. These women are dreamers. They began dreaming of becoming nationally accredited and they made the dream a reality. Jonnene McFarland, executive director of the Pueblo Zoo, is in her dream job. In fact, it seems that all three women are doing the exact kind of work that once made for daydreams and fantasies of little girls. McFarland has been actively involved with the Pueblo Zoo for sixteen years. She began her work at the Zoo as a volunteer docent and was later a program specialist for

the City of Pueblo assigned to the Zoo. Later, in 1991 when the Pueblo Zoological Society assumed management of the Zoo, McFarland was hired as executive director.

Marti Osborn is the associate director/education director of the zoo and is also the founding member of the Pueblo Zoological Society. Marti was also the zoo's first executive director and since then she and Jonnene McFarland have switched roles so that each of them is doing what they are best at. Osborn says that since college she's known that she wanted to be a biologist. "I have always wanted to help get the message across about the importance of saving habitat and animals." As education director for the zoo, Osborn has an opportunity to deliver that message to more than 14,000 school age children each year.

Marilyn McBirney, curator of the Pueblo Zoo, has been in Pueblo for the past two and one-half years. She was attracted to the small zoo because "number one it was in Colorado and because the zoo offered a tremendous challenge. When I found out that the zoo was attempting to become accredited, I wanted to be a part of that process."

The field of zoo keeping, curating and directing is a new frontier for women. "Most of the directors and curators were men. Now, there are a lot more women in all aspects of the field."

"The last two years have been a tremendous learning process. I have learned about things I never dreamed of. I do not know a lot of it well, but, I now know a little about tractors, hay, sewers, sprinkling systems and all those things you never think of," laughed McFarland.[8]

Marilyn Birney, Jonnie McFarland, and Marti Osborn in 1993.

(*Image courtesy of the Pueblo Zoological Society*)

---

[8] Cynthia Illick, "Dreaming a Zoo Come True," *Woman's Focus*, July, 1993, clipping in *Pueblo Zoo Album 1991-1992*, Pueblo City-County Library.

About this time, a youngster fell on Monkey Mountain and broke his arm. His grandmother fussed at him about being careful and staying on the path while they loaded him into an ambulance. But when the bills came, she changed her tune and contacted the Zoological Society's insurance company. Soon, Jonnie received a call from the agent, who said, "Close the Mountain. You have a 1930's structure in a 1990's litigious society." Much to the chagrin of area residents, the Mountain was ringed with fencing and "closed" signs.

The year 1993 brought yet another challenge. The US Department of Agriculture once again cited the facility. This time, it was a rather unusual situation. Golf balls hit toward hole 4 on the adjacent City Park Golf Course were flying into the hoofstock pens along the Zoo's south side. Fortunately, no animals suffered, and the City agreed to relocate the offending tee box.[9]

It was not surprising that one of the biggest challenges of operating the Zoo was having enough money to do a good job. Every summer found the Zoological Society working with local politicians to assure City and County allocations would continue to provide a large portion of the operating budget. For the remainder of the budget, the Society relied on contributions, grants, earned income at the gate, and profits from the sales of gifts and food. Limited to selling only candy and packaged snacks in the gift shop and outcompeted by the City's concession outside the Zoo grounds, in 1994 a mobile concession trailer was purchased and parked permanently near the Education Building.

The Watering Hole in 1995.

(*Image courtesy of the Pueblo Zoological Society*)

[9] "Feds Teed Off Over Errant Balls at Zoo," *The Pueblo Chieftain*, April 29, 1993.

The Woods in 1992.

(*Image courtesy of the Pueblo Zoological Society*)

The Woods in 2005.

(*Image courtesy of the Pueblo Zoological Society*)

At the time the Zoo came under Zoological Society management, other than lawn around the perimeter, the five welded-wire cages near the entrance had no landscaping and few interesting exhibits. Conrad, a very popular Andean condor, was gone, and except for a golden eagle, the rest were pheasants. Marilyn located bobcats, lynxes, great horned owls, and a fisher to replace the pheasants. After extensive landscaping and the addition of interactive graphics, the area became a temperate forest exhibit called The Woods.

The Mahlon T. White Discovery Room was given a facelift in 1995. It had been open for ten years and was beginning to look more than a little well used, although the "well used" part was exactly what we were hoping for. The Mahlon Thatcher White Foundation helped with a $10,000 grant for new carpet, paint, and refurbishing the exhibits. New exhibits included displays on veterinary care, ocean biofacts, animal skulls, and a small log house that became a tiny-tot-sized veterinary clinic, complete with small lab coats, backlit x-rays, a stethoscope, and stuffed-animal "patients."

Planning ahead for the eventual rehabilitation of the 60-year-old structures built by the WPA, the Zoological Society contracted with Janet McFarland Burlile for preparation of an application for their listing on the National Register of Historic Places.[10] If included, the structures would be eligible for grants from the State Historical Fund.[11] The application was successful, and listing of the structures together as the Pueblo Zoo Historic District was announced on August 29, 1995.

The Zoological Society launched a capital campaign in 1996 to begin improvements specified in the Zoo's third master plan: renovation of pens along the west perimeter into Grasslands of the World (Australian, South American, Asian, and North American animal species) and construction of a group picnic shelter. For the first Grasslands project, Johnson Station in the Australian Outback, the dividing fences between two pens were removed to enlarge an exhibit of kangaroos. Emus were introduced, and landscaping was added. One of two concrete animal shelters was kept and improved. The biggest challenge was a second shelter with a solid back wall only a few feet from the viewing sidewalk. Richard Montano turned it into a tumbledown shed on an Outback station by siding it with weathered wood and cutting a large opening near the sidewalk for visitor entry. He enclosed much of the open side that faced into the exhibit, installing heavy wire mesh in a big hole through which visitors could enjoy the animals.

As work was progressing at Johnson Station, we, the authors, had an adventure that could have turned expensive or even worse, tragic. Board Member Reg Landrum had given the Zoo a used dump truck. Although it was old, it was in good condition. The two of us decided we needed genuine latillas to make a screening fence along the front side of the exhibit.[12] Having ordered a truckload of latillas from a source in Taos, New Mexico, we climbed into the trusty (we thought) dump truck and headed off on the 350-mile round trip that involved a mountain pass and winding roads. The trip to Taos went well, we loaded up the latillas, headed back to Pueblo, and arrived safely. A few days

---

[10] Animal House, Tropical Bird House, Monkey Island, (Old) Bear Pits, stone lampposts, and stone walls
[11] The State Historical Fund was created by the 1990 constitutional amendment allowing limited gaming in the towns of Black Hawk, Central City, and Cripple Creek. The amendment directs that a portion of the gaming tax revenues be used for historic preservation throughout the state. <https://www.historycolorado.org/state-historical-fund>
[12] Latillas are peeled branches laid between the beams of a ceiling.

later we told Reg about our trip. He was alarmed, saying he never intended for the old truck to be taken out of town. That was disconcerting, but not nearly as much as when we discovered the City's liability insurance on the Zoo's vehicles only covered them while in Colorado. As soon as we crossed into New Mexico, we were driving without insurance, which could have resulted in a stiff fine or, even worse, the consequences of an accident. We seemed to be experts at learning the hard way!

Another project during 1993 was the renovation of what was called the waterfowl area, several acres that the Parks Department had developed into canals and islands in the 1960s. Each year from March 15 to November 15, the enormous amount of water needed to fill the canals came from the Bessemer Ditch.[13] During the winter months, to give ducks and geese a safe retreat from birds of prey or the occasional wild fox that might sneak into the area, it was necessary to keep open water in the canals surrounding one of the islands. Opening two frost-proof hydrants and letting them run almost continuously for four months accomplished this; however, the Board of Water Works realized this was a tremendous volume of treated water that they were supplying without charge to the Zoo. They insisted that usage be reduced. After securing grants and in-kind work, the canals were dredged, gabions were restored, an aeration system was installed, and concrete dams were built at the inlet and outlet. Bentonite was added along the dammed side to decrease seepage.[14] Filling with treated water was still required whenever ditch water was unavailable, but the amount was greatly reduced.

The waterfowl ponds and islands had a lot of potential, but were extremely challenging to manage.

(*Image courtesy of the Pueblo Zoological Society*)

[13] The City owns the water rights, an important consideration under Colorado water law.
[14] Sodium bentonite swells on contact with water, making it useful for sealing irrigation ditches.

In 1996, the Zoological Society received a Community Development Block Grant to fund the addition of a second fence along Parkside Lane on the west side of the Zoo. During the 1930s, a low rock wall and a moat (ditch) were built along this street to contain bison and elk. Over the years, more hoofstock pens were built along the ditch. That the animals had access to the untreated water did not meet 1980s USDA standards for animal health. The City was required to build a fence that blocked animal access to the water. In winter it was relatively easy for vandals to climb the low wall and enter the Zoo by walking through the seasonally dry ditch, however. Building the second fence greatly increased the security of the entire grounds.

The capital campaign had raised enough to fund construction of the Mandari picnic shelter in 1997. The Zoological Society planned to raise funds for Zoo operation by using the large shelter to expand the annual Zoofari fund raising event and through rentals for group picnics of up to 250 persons. Within the next few years, income from rentals became an important part of the Zoo's budget.

The origin of the name Mandari is a mystery.

(*Image courtesy of the Pueblo Zoological Society*)

That year, too, it was time to build sun bear Solar Sue a really spacious new exhibit in the Asian Adventure section of the Grasslands. And, because the public kept asking for more monkeys, the Zoological Society decided to include a habitat for Sulawesi macaques. A 900-square-foot central holding building connected to two 1,200-square-foot outdoor exhibit areas was built for the two species. Clifford Taylor Architects designed the exhibit, Bret Verna (BAV Construction) built it, and Richard Montano fabricated rockwork in both exhibits.

When we accepted Sulawesi macaques for the Asian Adventure exhibit, we did not realize the implications of their testing positive for the Hepatitis B virus. Because the liver inflammation caused by Hepatis B is potentially fatal in humans, for their protection zookeepers were required to be vaccinated and wear protective clothing, goggles, and face shields each time they entered the holding building. After a few years of devoting more resources to the species than it was financially prudent for our small zoo to provide, we transferred the monkeys to the Denver Zoo. White-handed gibbons, Suzie and Rocket, replaced them. Gibbons, although tailless, are apes that closely resemble monkeys.

Work toward future rehabilitation of structures in the Pueblo Zoo Historic District continued in 1998 when Clifford Taylor Architects completed a master plan for the area. The following year Keith Larson (Jones & Jones, Seattle), Bob Hart (HGF Architects, Pueblo), and Parry Thomas (Thomas & Thomas, Colorado Springs) developed concept plans for the Monkey Mountain, Animal House, Monkey Island, and the adjoining 2.5 acres.

For nearly ten years, the animal care and maintenance staffs had been housed in the Commissary, a modified house with only a poorly equipped animal examination room. By 1998 staff and animal care needs had outgrown this small building. An appeal, headed by long-time supporters Dr. Joe

Sulawesi macaque monkey.

(*Image courtesy of the McBirney Family*)

and Sidney Clutter and Dr. Mark and Carol Rickman, resulted in significant support from the medical community. On August 12, 1998, ground was broken for a single-story addition, a new second story, and a 2-story-tall stall for the treatment and isolation of large hoofstock. Designed by HGF Architects, the new facility included animal examination, surgery, quarantine, and necropsy rooms, curator and grounds management offices, and a larger staff break room.

Donors to Grasslands of the World and the Mandari group picnic shelter were recognized on the "Penny Python," draped over the top of a wall where donors' names are engraved on a copper plate. Mahlon "Butch" and Maylan White, as well as the Mahlon Thatcher White Foundation underwrote Richard's work.[15] The python is twenty feet long, weighs 110 pounds, and is made of 8,756 pennies, a part of the 246,946 collected by Pueblo's school children during the Ecocenter "Pennies for Penguins" drive.

It took Richard Montano 1,300 hours over eight months to fabricate a copper mesh covered armature and then solder the pennies to it with their Lincoln heads all pointing in the same direction. The "Penny Python's" head was sculpted in clay and cast in bronze.

(*Image courtesy of Katy McDonald*)

---

[15] "Penny Python Will Grace Pueblo Zoo's Donor Wall," *The Pueblo Chieftain*, March 8, 2001.

In the midst of all the improvements and construction, the Zoological Society struggled to address concerns about the need for more money to operate the Zoo properly and to maintain its accreditation. In 1989, voters in Denver and surrounding counties had approved a dedicated sales tax for the Scientific and Cultural Facilities District (SCFD) that turned the metro area into a major cultural center by providing an assured base of funding and allowing the top tier facilities such as the Denver Zoo, along with many smaller organizations, to thrive and to expand. By 1998, the Zoological Society decided that it was time to try something similar for the Pueblo Zoo and some of Pueblo's other local nonprofits. Representatives of the Society's Board and staff therefore consulted with political pollster and Pueblo native Floyd Ciruli, who together with Denver Zoo Director Clayton Freiheit had successfully designed and implemented the Denver campaign. He told us frankly that it would not work in Pueblo, but in typical perhaps foolhardy fashion we went ahead anyway. Society Board member Rick McIlroy and former City Councilman Chris Weaver co-chaired the campaign that included Rosemount Museum, Sangre de Cristo Arts and Conference Center, Pueblo Railway Museum, Weisbrod Aircraft Museum, Nature Center of Pueblo, and the Pueblo Symphony. City Council declined the opportunity to put the measure on an upcoming ballot, and so the organizations forged ahead with acquiring signatures to get initiatives on the ballot to establish the district and levy a small sales tax.

During the summer of 1999, petitions in hand, a small group of us gathered signatures at every possible local event. We stood in front of grocery stores and discount houses, finally securing enough signatures for the County's citizens to consider the measure in the November election. The issue failed, but of course we had been warned! The loss was not nearly as bad as losing Chris Weaver to a massive heart attack the morning after the election. He had tried so hard to make it possible for our community to benefit from a cultural tax, and we all were completely devastated.

As it moved into the new millennium, the Zoological Society continued in-house work on the Grasslands theme for the hoofstock pens on the west side of the Zoo by creating the South American Pampas for maned wolves, a Colorado Short Grass Prairie exhibit of bison and elk, and the Asian Steppes to house Przewalski's Asian wild horses. At the Asian Steppes, a modern canvas yurt was converted into a Mongolian *ger* that visitors could enter to view the horses though a clear panel.

That same year, the Mahlon Thatcher White Foundation gifted "Lola," a bronze rabbit sculpture by Loveland, Colorado sculptor Dan Ostermiller. A year later, the Foundation gave the Zoo another Ostermiller bronze, "Bear Pause," that was situated in a shady spot near the North American Prairie exhibit. The installation of safety surfaces under each of the sculptures was funded by donations in memory of Doris Stillman and Jonnie's mother, Irene Dunlop.

After the Malayan sun bear Solar Sue was moved to her new home in the Asian Adventure, upgrades were made in 2001 to her previous exhibit on the south side of Monkey Mountain, and red pandas were moved into it. Richard Montano built a second cage for Asian tragopans (also called horned pheasants). The viewing area was decorated with bamboo rails, fencing, and an ornate sign that announced "Asian Mountain."

The next year Richard was commissioned to replace an outdoor drinking fountain that the Parks Department had installed in the Zoo sometime in the 1970s. It was a large, plastic lion head with its

Logos drawn by Richard Montano for Pueblo's cultural facilities.

(*Image courtesy of the Pueblo Zoological Society*)

At the North American Prairie exhibit of bison and elk new graphics, paths, landscaping, fencing, and a tipi were added, while the animal shelters were disguised as sod houses used by settlers on the Great Plains.

(*Images courtesy of the Pueblo Zoological Society and Andi Apodaca*)

"Bear Pause."

(*Image courtesy of the Pueblo Zoological Society*)

Kids love sharing a drink with a tiny lion cub.

(*Image courtesy of the Pueblo Zoological Society*)

Pictured (*left to right*) at the otter exhibit groundbreaking on March 4, 2003, are major donors Peggy Capek, Marion Guerrero and, Ruth Robinson, as well as Mahlon "Butch" and Maylan White (Mahlon Thatcher White Foundation), Randy Thurston (City Council), Betty Wilkinson (major donor), Larry Moore (major in-kind donor), and Mark Carmel (Pueblo County).

(*Image courtesy of the Pueblo Zoological Society*)

mouth wide open. Kids loved sticking their heads into the big cat's huge mouth for a drink. Worn out, it was removed, although not forgotten by visitors. Richard balked at fabricating another lion with gaping mouth, saying he thought kids were getting the wrong message by sticking their heads into the mouth of a dangerous animal. Instead, for an area near the African lion exhibit, he created a bronze lion cub atop a rock outcropping sculpted in fiberglass.

The Zoo's next major project was construction of a river otter exhibit, for which it had taken seven years of dedication to secure funding. In 1996, Marti joined the Pueblo Natural Resources and Environmental Education Council and faithfully attended each of their meetings until 2003, when the exhibit became part of the Arkansas River Corridor Legacy Project, which received major financial support from a Great Outdoors Colorado Legacy Grant. Matching funds were pledged by the City and Pueblo County, as well as by numerous Zoo supporters.

A shelter shades the south-facing glass viewing windows of the river otter exhibit.

(*Image courtesy of the Pueblo Zoological Society*)

The river otter exhibit features underwater viewing of this semi-aquatic species and realistic rockwork, as well as a waterfall and a stream. Adjoining the exhibit, a holding building contains animal night cages, as well as the pumps, filters, and ozone generation equipment required to keep the pool water clean and clear.[16] Behind the building, a large off-exhibit outdoor pen provides a second space for animal management. Opened on July 12, 2003, the exhibit was an instant success with the public, receiving a 2004 Regional Starburst Award for the creative and cost-efficient use of Lottery funds, the economic and social impact of the project, and community participation.

In order to increase the number of out-of-town visitors to the Zoo, they had to be able to find the place. Signs did lead the way through city streets, but there were none on the interstate highway. Through the persistence of Zoological Society Board member Diana Johnson, both the State and the City put signs on I-25 at either end of the city as well as some leading to the west entrance of City Park along eastbound highway 50 and both south and north bound Pueblo Boulevard. At the Pueblo Boulevard and Goodnight Avenue entrance to City Park, however, there was no indication that the Zoo was inside the park. Board member Larry Moore volunteered to build a tall brick structure at the corner, Richard Montano created artwork to be installed on it, Summit Brick donated bricks, the Parks Department gave its blessing, and the electric utility hooked up a light.

The largest capital improvement during our tenure was undoubtedly the rehabilitation of the historic Animal House and adjoining Monkey Island, which happened between 1999 and 2007.

---

[16] Zoological Society Board of Directors member Larry Moore of Larry's Electric and Refrigeration laid all of the concrete block for the otter holding building without charge to the Zoo.

Standing at the west entrance to Pueblo's City Park, the brick sign is adorned with a majestic bronze lion head, sculpted by Richard Montano.

(*Image courtesy of the Pueblo Zoological Society*)

Because the scope of this project was vastly more challenging and complex than any other with which we were involved, we have chosen to tell its particular story in the following chapter.

While our small staff was guiding work at the Animal House and Monkey Island, we were handed yet another challenge! During, a routine inspection late in 2005, the USDA dealt the Zoo quite a blow by citing the Happy Time Ranch for inadequate fencing. The citation stated that for the animals' safety the goats, sheep, rabbits, horses, donkeys, and llamas must be fenced from human contact unless trained personnel were present, a staffing cost that the Zoo's lean budget could not afford. So, after much moaning, groaning and discussion, the Zoological Society decided to make the best of it, and early the next year raised $50,000 to completely renovate the exhibit. All fences were replaced and new rabbit and chicken pens were built. Half of the little barn was converted into a pig exhibit, with the rest becoming a walk-through display of farm equipment. New installations included a hand-washing station, a child-sized hatched eggshell made of concrete, a farm animal photo area, a real covered wagon, and a new entrance. We developed an area that could be opened when staff was present to allow visitors to feed and interact with goats and sheep. Volunteer Babe Pinelle redecorated the interior of the little farmhouse, while staff member Jim Pinelle outfitted the blacksmith shop. Long the centerpiece of the Zoo and beloved by generations of young children, the area's new name became Pioneer Ranch. In the end, remodeling the area 45 years after it was built turned out to be a joy rather than a chore!

Entrance to the Pioneer Ranch.
*(Image courtesy of the
Pueblo Zoological Society)*

The goat pen showing new log fences
and animal shelters.
(Image courtesy of the Pueblo Zoological Society)

Brooke and Nicole Guarienti at photo area
with covered wagon in the background.
(Image courtesy of the Pueblo Zoological Society)

Gwendolyn Osborn in a giant concrete eggshell.

(Image courtesy of the Pueblo Zoological Society)

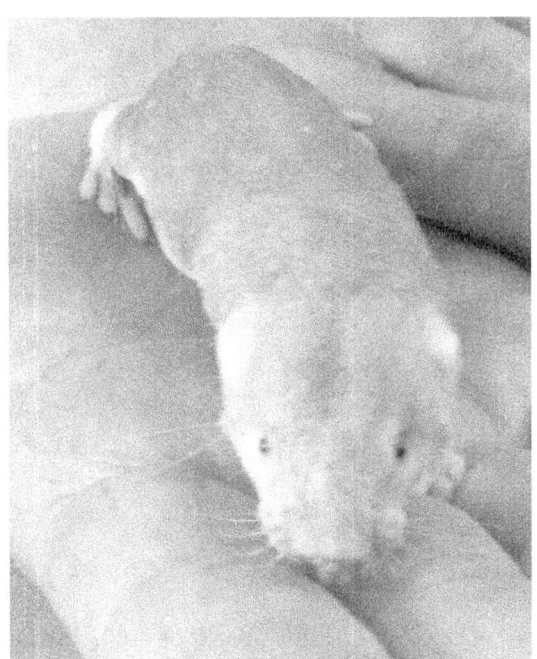

The naked mole-rat (*Heterocephalus glaber*), a small East African rodent that is resistant to cancer, cannot feel pain, and may live for 32 years, is not only interesting to watch, but also affords a wealth of interpretive information.

(*Image courtesy of the Pueblo Zoological Society*)

Two new animal exhibits were added in 2008. One featured some tiny animals that are so ugly they are cute. Naked mole rats are indeed rats with no hair, except for a few whiskers and a little hair on their feet. These little pink-skinned critters caught the fancy of Alan and Percan Polivka, who made a generous contribution to build the exhibit. Richard Montano created and installed a system of tubes and nest boxes in the hallway between the rainforest and penguin areas of the Ecocenter, and it was not long until the busy little rodents captured the hearts of visitors.

The second new exhibit was built for cotton-top tamarins, small New World primates with long white crests atop their heads. Richard Montano fabricated and installed naturalistic fiberglass trees and vines in an enclosed space within the Ecocenter rainforest. This allowed interpretation of the role this species plays in tropical rainforests, while meeting health and safety standards for both the animals and the viewing public.

A long list of other new projects kept everyone busy. Two educational displays were installed in the Discovery Room, as well as others of Pueblo County insects, reptiles, and wildflowers in various indoor locations. A barn owl exhibit was built in the Pioneer Ranch stable.[17] To increase the energy efficiency of the facility, solar panels were placed on the Animal Care Center, hay barn, and lion holding building, while all lighting was retrofitted with energy efficient lamps. Two additional walk-in freezers were installed to store large shipments of meat and fish for the animals. General Curator Marilyn McBirney and the zookeepers initiated an animal training program that would

---

[17] The miniature stable was built about 1989 by a Parks Department crew, who named it after their supervisor, Chet Akers. A plaque on the barn reads: C. Akers Homestead, Population 1, Elevation 4712 ½ ft.

In the World of Color, bird exhibits replaced the diorama.
One of the "colorful" graphic displays can be seen on the left.

(*Image courtesy of the Pueblo Zoological Society*)

The first building in the "African Village," housing food concession and public restrooms, was not officially opened until after we both retired in July 2012.

(*Image courtesy of the Pueblo Zoological Society*)

teach some of the animals to cooperate in daily routines, demonstrate natural behaviors, and assist in their own veterinary care. A complete facilities survey was done to document water and sewer mains, electric and gas lines, irrigation backflow valves, and drainage patterns. To our knowledge, this type of comprehensive documentation had not previously been done for the Zoo's twenty-five acres. We hoped it would facilitate future planning as the Zoological Society worked to develop exciting new exhibits and visitor conveniences.

In addition to several smaller projects completed in 2009, a new viewing area was built for the North American Prairie exhibit of bison and elk, animal management fencing was installed around the Savannah Barn, and the Cold-Blooded Creatures herpetarium was updated into the World of Color, which allowed an endless number of concepts to be interpreted. When the building was re-opened, it still was primarily an exhibit of reptiles and amphibians, but now with the addition of colorful birds.

The Zoological Society kicked off a $2.5 million capital campaign in 2010 to fund construction of a black rhinoceros exhibit, a food concession and restrooms in a simulated African village, and a wildlife-learning center. Preliminary plans called for the rhinoceros exhibit and food concession to be located in a large unused area south of the lion exhibit. Once the first funds were raised, the project began with the installation of the water, sewer, and electrical lines needed for the rhinoceros exhibit and the development of architectural plans for the food concession building by WDM Architects of Wichita, Kansas.

Early in 2011, we both announced that we were ready to retire, and although we probably should have been winding down, we did not. Construction of the food concession building was started. Improvements to the Education Building were made, and the two of us kept everyone overly busy! Once again, a large notebook of accreditation materials had to be readied for submission to the AZA early in 2012, a task that required work on the part of many of the Zoo's staff. Curator Marilyn McBirney introduced three new animal exhibits: bald eagles, tiny Kirk's dik-dik, and Sichuan takin (a large goat-like species related to sheep).

Chapter Four

Animal House & Monkey Island Become Islands of Life

Transformation of the historic Animal House and adjoining Monkey Island into what would be called the Islands of Life presented the Pueblo Zoological Society with countless inspiring opportunities and many unique challenges. Requiring $3.2 million and thirteen years, it was no doubt the largest and most complex project undertaken by the Society after the non-profit assumed management of the Pueblo Zoo.

The story begins in 1994 with the Society's successful application for listing of the Pueblo Zoo Historic District on the National Register of Historic Places. A master plan was developed for the entire Historic District in 1998, soon followed by concept plans for the rehabilitation of Monkey Mountain, the Animal House, and Monkey Island.

An attempt in 2000 to raise the $5 million needed to rehabilitate Monkey Mountain, the Animal House, and Monkey Island failed, primarily because the public was less than excited about the initial project. Those who remembered the challenge of climbing the Mountain as children felt that required safety modifications would take all the fun out of the experience. Within a year, the campaign was altered by removing the Mountain project, instead focusing on only the Animal House and adjoining Monkey Island, plus site improvements and landscaping for the 2.5-acre area surrounding both features.

The State Historical Fund required and funded an historic structures assessment, which was necessary for consideration of a grant proposal for the rehabilitation of the exterior of the Animal House, its historic artwork, and the structures on Monkey Island. Nan Anderson (Andrews & Anderson, Golden, Colorado) completed the assessment in 2002.

In the meantime, the capital campaign was kicked off by a $500,000 grant from the David and Lucile Packard Foundation. In the ensuing years, the Zoological Society received a $343,425 grant from the State Historical Fund, grants from the Mahlon Thatcher White and other foundations, commitments from both the City and the County, and contributions, pledges and in-kind donations from individuals and corporations. A program that gave the capital campaign a big boost was expansion of the Pueblo Urban Enterprise Zone to allow donors to the Zoo to claim significant state tax credits.[1] The capital campaign was completed in 2005 when challenge grants were claimed from the Gates Family Foundation and the Boettcher Foundation.

Over 60 years old, the shipwrecked *Ada Mae* and the lighthouse on Monkey Island were decrepit. The Animal House was old, dismal, smelly, and even haunted according to some zookeepers. When the Zoological Society assumed management of the Zoo in 1991, half of the Animal House cages were empty. Visitor satisfaction demanded the empty cages be occupied, however, because the building was the Zoo's primary indoor exhibit space. So as soon as General Curator Marilyn McBirney came on board, she began acquiring animals for the exhibits, always keeping in mind the goal of emptying them again within a few years. Animals were chosen carefully. Some, such as the black-footed ferrets, were selected because they were nearing the end of their lifespans. The fennec foxes were acquired because it would be easy to find new homes for them. Some species, including lemurs and meerkats, were to be held off-exhibit for display when new exhibits were ready for them. By the end of 1999, the building had been emptied.

For many, closing the Animal House was an emotional experience. The building's last zookeeper wrote,

> The animals are relocated and the building no longer rings with children's squeals as the lemurs bounce off the walls in anticipation of the day's food selection. There is no longer a daily keeper routine with tasks specialized for the needs of the small mammals whose home this has been for many years. No more dusting the window sills, nor cleaning the windows …

---

[1] The Pueblo Zoo was not in the approved geographic area, but when Pueblo banker Mike Matthews, a Colorado Economic Development Commissioner, took up the cause, the zone was expanded on October 23, 2004. Persons who contribute $250 or more to a nonprofit in an Enterprise Zone within a year can claim a 25% Colorado State income tax credit.

> I cannot hope to give anyone more than a glimpse, a snapshot of a few moments meaningful to me as a keeper and as a person—a reminder to respect the forms and boundaries of life, for in the history of the earth, all that is or ever has been seems to be … just passing through.[2]

Zoological consultant Keith Larson of Jones and Jones (Seattle) came on board to develop a theme for the animal exhibits. After much study and deliberation, the planning committee chose Islands of Life as both the overall theme and as the new name for the Animal House.[3] The concept was to include not only oceanic island species, but also species isolated by other geographic barriers.

One of the first requirements was to make the entire Pueblo Zoo Historic District more accessible from the rest of the Zoo. The 1930s structures were built to face a street that ran along the north side of the Animal House. Newer exhibits and facilities were built on the south side of a wide moat (canal) that ran behind the building. Once the street was removed and perimeter fencing built, reaching the Animal House was complicated for visitors. To correct this problem, a bridge was built over the canal and a doorway was cut into the building's south wall. To provide a firm foundation for the bridge, the crumbling canal banks were stabilized with concrete walls.

The new bridge to Islands of Life.

(*Image courtesy of the Pueblo Zoological Society*)

---

[2] *Pueblo ZooNews*, December 1999, *Pueblo Zoo Album 1999-2000*, Pueblo City-County Library.

[3] A great planning committee stayed with the project for the entire eight years. As well as General Curator Marilyn McBirney and the two of us, it included Richard Montano, Board members Mike Blazer and Larry Moore, Buildings and Grounds Supervisor Jim Pinelle, and Bob Hart, HGF Architects. Contractors were BAV Construction, Ark Valley Construction, Dodson Studios (Virginia), and Thomas & Thomas (Colorado Springs).

Restored doors on the north side of the Animal House.

(*Image courtesy of the Pueblo Zoological Society*)

While the bridge was under construction, exterior restoration of the Animal House began and included stonework repair, window and roof replacement, and removal of the barred big-cat cages from the south face of the structure. Inside the building, the ceiling and walls of the historic central cupola were repaired and painted by the contractor, while Richard Montano restored the historic drinking fountain. He also restored the bas-relief in one of the cages that was preserved to showcase the quality of the artwork done by a Works Progress Administration artist. Restoration of the building also required removal of metal-framed glass doors that had long ago been substituted for the original wooden entry doors on the north side of the Animal House. The preservation plan called for their replacement with doors more closely resembling the original ones, while still complying with modern requirements for accessibility and safety.

As the unique historical features of the structures were being brought back to their original condition, Richard Montano restored the shipwrecked *Ada Mae* and the lighthouse on Monkey Island. Because only one of the monkey sculptures that once guarded the east door of the building had survived and was in very poor condition, Richard sculpted new ones out of concrete. He also repaired and repainted the lion, bear, and gorilla sculptures that stood atop the Animal House cupola. In the process of removing many layers of paint applied through the years, Richard discovered that they originally had been painted to represent the major metals found in Colorado—gold, silver, and copper. He painted each in its original color, the lion in gold, the gorilla in silver, and the bear in copper.

The *Ada Mae* with her mast, cabin, and name replaced.

(*Image courtesy of the Pueblo Zoological Society*)

The lantern room at the top of the lighthouse was restored,
with its light rewired and made functional once again.

(*Image courtesy of the Pueblo Zoological Society*)

Richard Montano repaints the lion atop the Animal House.

(*Image courtesy of The Pueblo Chieftain*)

Richard Montano's design drawing of the reticulated python and meerkat exhibits.

(*Image courtesy of Pueblo Zoological Society*)

This photograph of the Islands of Life west wing shows the completed alligator snapping turtle pool in a mangrove swamp (*left*) and the Rodrigues Island fruit bat exhibit (*right*).

(*Image courtesy of the Pueblo Zoological Society*)

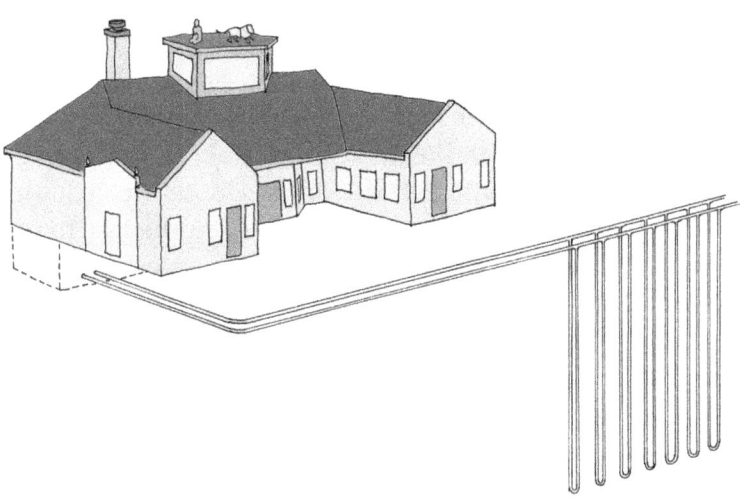

Richard Montano's drawing shows the location of the geothermal wells in relation to the Islands of Life building.

(*Image courtesy of the Pueblo Zoological Society*)

After the Animal House had been completely gutted, zoological consultant Keith Larson worked with architect Bob Hart to design the physical layout of the cages, while architect Kelton Osborn developed a palette of colors for paint and carpeting in the visitor areas to complement the living exhibits and informational graphics. Richard Montano drew plans for each of the exhibits and their "furniture" of sculpted trees, cliffs, and rocks.[4] Unfortunately, Keith Larson passed away before completion of the plans, so we were on our own without his expert guidance.

One means of meeting the Islands of Life project's goal of energy efficiency was installation of a state-of-the art geothermal system to heat and cool the building. With advice from Sarah Porter Osborn, the Society received a grant from the StEPP Foundation to fund installation of the system by drilling twenty-four geothermal wells and installing heating and cooling equipment inside the building.[5]

Planning an exhibit to occupy the center of the Animal House under the historic cupola proved to be one of the hardest tasks and a test of the planning committee's creativity. The first idea, presented by zoological consultant Keith Larson, was an open exhibit with two ponds: mudskippers in one, fiddler crabs in the other. The two of us headed to the Denver Zoo to observe mudskippers. They are very interesting little critters, but perhaps not ones that would impress visitors as they first entered the building. Next, we bought some fiddler crabs and tried to keep them alive in the Discovery Room. That did not work well at all. Back to the proverbial drawing board we went. As a second choice, we settled on Komodo dragons, an excellent island representative. This time we took General Curator Marilyn McBirney, Buildings and Grounds Supervisor Jim Pinelle, and architect Bob Hart along to the Denver Zoo. We learned all about how to build exhibits for the species, but then we smelled them! It was back to the drawing board once again. Larry Moore, a long-time Zoological Society board member, suggested we build a sailing ship. Envisioned as an educational display, the committee hoped it would elicit a great deal of creativity from Zoo visitors as they imagined the story of its daring voyages to new lands.

Richard Montano was excited about the idea, but he had never built a ship. For this reason, we sent him to the Maritime Museum of San Diego to study the HMS *Surprise*, the tall ship featured in the movie *Master and Commander: The Far Side of the World*.[6] He spent many hours aboard, carefully photographing and measuring everything. When he returned, he told us that the real ship was so large that only part of it would fit inside the building. He suggested that he build a shipwreck, broken apart in a storm, with about a third of it beached on a faraway island. That third, the stern, would contain the captain's quarters as well as a small cargo area with space for a few exhibits for small animals. At the building's opening celebration, the ship would be christened the *Thatcher*,

---

[4] Since the 1980s, Richard Montano had done virtually all of the Zoo's concrete sculptural work. Because he was working on so many other projects at both the Animal House and Monkey Island, he did not have time for this work. Instead, Dodson Studios (Virginia) were contracted to complete the sculptural work, according to Richard's designs and under his supervision.

[5] In short, the StEPP Foundation facilitates project identification when an entity chooses to resolve an environmental law violation through a negotiated regulatory settlement agreement that has tangible benefits to the affected community.

[6] The HMS *Surprise* is a genuine sailing ship originally built in 1970 as the HMS *Rose* and based on 18th-century drawings of a 1757 frigate.

Richard Montano building the *Thatcher*.
(*Image courtesy of the Pueblo Zoological Society*)

in honor of Mahlon "Butch" White, long-time Zoo benefactor and president of the Mahlon Thatcher White Foundation.

It took Richard most of 2006 and 2007 to build the *Thatcher*. He constructed the main structure in his studio, dismantled it, reassembled it in the atrium of the building, added a mast and torn sails, and then painted its colorful exterior. Most of the upper structure of the ship was built of wood salvaged when the Pioneer Ranch was being updated. The sails were made from canvas saved when a worn out tipi at the North American exhibit was replaced.

Of course, the story of the Pueblo Zoo's *Thatcher* is purely imaginary. Employing much creative license, it is based loosely on the voyages of the eighteenth and nineteenth centuries when "voyages around the world had no other goal than to obtain new information about geography, the natural sciences, and the mores of different peoples."[7] Because, there is space in the shipwreck's stern for only the captain's quarters, that area had to serve not only as a space for the fictional captain, but also for the display of the artifacts and specimens collected by the imaginary scientist on-board. This may seem to imply that the captain was a scientist, something that was not true on historic voyages of discovery. Zoo visitors can look through windows into the captain's quarters to find furnishings, supplies, and navigational tools along with many surprises. They learn that the voyagers found fossils, new species of animals and plants, and traded for artifacts from islanders they encountered. It is up to the imaginations of visitors to determine how long ago the *Thatcher* wrecked, although it was long enough so only the skeleton of the captain remains. Some real animals have moved in, while some that the explorers collected have survived and made themselves at home in the cargo area.

Marti tells how the displays in the *Thatcher* were developed at a cost the project's limited budget could bear.

---

[7] Jacques Brosse, *Great Voyages of Discovery, Circumnavigators and Scientists 1764-1843*, preface by Fernand Braudel, translated by Stanley Hochman (New York, N.Y. : Facts on File Publications, 1983), 7.

Stern of the *Thatcher* with windows into the captain's quarters.

(*Image courtesy of the Pueblo Zoological Society*)

The port side of the *Thatcher* – Richard made the cannon from a discarded fire extinguisher. The nets were made by a professional net fabricator and volunteer on the HMS *Surprise* in San Diego.

(*Image courtesy of the Pueblo Zoological Society*)

The captain's desk appears to have been used by someone who has been recording scientific discoveries.

(*Image courtesy of the Pueblo Zoological Society*)

The poor captain lies permanently at rest in a hammock. His naval jacket, pants, and shirt were created by retired costume designer Jeanette Ball, a long-time Zoo cashier.

(*Image courtesy of Steven McDonald*)

Jonnie and I had a very rewarding time studying sailing history books to learn what the voyagers might have collected. We asked retired Development Assistant Pat Ponce to explore the frigate USS *Constellation* on display in the Baltimore harbor. There she learned our captain might have had a bathtub in his quarters, so we included one made from a very old metal laundry tub used many years earlier by Jonnie's mother. We made numerous on-line orders for such items as historic navigational tools and biological specimens. After scouring antique shops in Pueblo, Florence, and Denver, we headed to Bent's Fort near La Junta where the blacksmith gave us hand wrought, square-headed nails. As we gathered items to display, Steven McDonald, Senior Instructor/Technical Director in the University of Colorado Boulder's Theatre Department, led an independent study for five undergraduate students in the Design and Technology program. The students identified furnishings that might have been found aboard ship and then crafted several pieces, including the desk, table, and a painted floorcloth. They designed the layout and installed both the furnishings and the items we had obtained.[8]

As word spread about the work being done to rehabilitate the Animal House, quite a few people popped into our office to tell us about a beautiful fountain that was once in the central area under the cupola. It was said to have featured three very shiny black seals and other smaller creatures. As larger cages were built for the lions and tigers, the fountain was buried under dirt and a thick concrete cage floor. George R. Williams told us that he thought the seals were worth saving, but after so many years it seemed even George could not recall exactly where it had been. The building contractor tried in vain to find the fountain before the new concrete floor was poured. Our crew—Richard Montano, Jim Pinelle, John Alderton, and Richard Valdez—took over and began to dig. They dug and dug, but found nothing. Just as they were about to give up, Zoological Society board member John Ercul came into our office. Upon hearing about our challenge, he grabbed pen and paper, drawing the seals as he remembered them as an 8-year-old. With a few more hours of digging, his drawing led to the discovery of the seals. Removing the extremely heavy sculpture from the deep pit was another problem, solved by the expertise of our maintenance crew and borrowed heavy equipment. The head of one of the seals had been cut off when the floor was poured for the cat cages, but was able to be repaired during the restoration process.

Seals at time of discovery.

Seals following restoration.

(*Images courtesy of the Pueblo Zoological Society*)

---

[8] Personal communication, Martha "Marti" Osborn.

Bali Mynah.
(Indonesia)

Rodrigues Island Fruit Bats.
(Mauritius)

San Esteban Island Chuckwallas.
(Gulf of California)

Ring-tailed lemurs.
(Madagascar)

*(All images courtesy of
Pueblo Zoological Society)*

Most the animals for the Islands of Life habitats were chosen to represent various kinds of islands, as can be seen in the names of some from oceanic islands. Some of the species were chosen because they represent kinds of isolated habitats other than oceanic islands, however. African rock hyraxes live on isolated rock kopjes or small hills isolated in generally flat areas. South American common squirrel monkeys represent islands of trees, which sometimes occur when meandering rivers cause sections of tropical rainforests to become isolated. For some of the animal acquisitions it was hard to stick to the theme. While not strictly an island species, a reticulated python was acquired because visitors wanted to see a ***really big*** snake.

Beyond interpretation of the species and their relationship to islands, educational graphics were developed to tell stories of island formation and of human cultures and their effect on the islands they inhabited or visited. Artifacts brought from Madagascar by Curator Marilyn McBirney and photographs of Easter Island taken by Educator Mary Tucey were incorporated into displays and graphics. A life-size cutout of an extinct Elephant Bird, once found on the island of Madagascar, illustrated the extreme vulnerability of island species.

Landscaping the approximately 2.5 acres around the building was yet another challenge. In the interest of water conservation, a primarily xeriscape design was chosen. Marti, wearing her metaphorical horticulturist hat, took over, purchasing the plants and overseeing in-house staff in their installation. For the Zoo's youngest visitors, a playground includes a small climbing wall and a giant rope spiderweb.[9]

When the work was finished and the animals had adjusted to their new homes, dignitaries and donors cut a ribbon to open the building, and then the Zoological Society Board of Directors hosted an evening celebration inside the building. Unfortunately, there was a big snowstorm in much of Colorado on April 12, 2007, the day of the opening party. The highways to the north of Pueblo were nearly impassable, making it impossible for some of the guests from that area to attend the opening.

Islands of Life could not have proceeded from vision to reality without the support of hundreds of donors. The names of those contributing to the capital campaign were recognized on tiles beside a 31-foot long relief sculpture created by Richard Montano. The artwork features more than sixty black, white, or black and white animals. Dubbed the Animural, it was installed on a 13-foot tall, 105-foot long wall built by Society Board member Larry Moore.[10]

Islands of Life received a 2008 Starburst Award for excellent use of Colorado Lottery Funds and a Historic Preservation Award from the Pueblo County Historical Society.

Common squirrel monkey.

(*Image courtesy of the Pueblo Zoological Society*)

---

[9] The playground was dedicated in memory of community leader Mike Stillman and the Zoo's beloved bookkeeper, Betty Kolesarek.

[10] The wall was built in an attempt to hide the sounds emanating from an indoor shooting range that is located literally just feet outside the Zoo.

By spring 2007, landscaping and concrete work were nearly completed.

(*Image courtesy of John Wark Photography, Pueblo Zoological Society collection*)

Mary Gunn from the David and Lucile Packard Foundation, County Commissioner Jeff Chostner, and City Councilwoman Judy Weaver were among those cutting the ribbon to officially open Islands of Life.

(*Image courtesy of the Pueblo Zoological Society*)

Maylan White, Mahlon Thatcher "Butch" White, Jonnie McFarland, Marti Osborn, and Capital Campaign Chair Carol Rickman.

(*Image courtesy of Tammy Guarienti, Pueblo Zoological Society Collection*)

Maylan White "christens" the *Thatcher* with a confetti-filled theatrical prop, while Mahlon Thatcher "Butch" White is ready for a champagne toast.

(*Image courtesy of Tammy Guarienti, Pueblo Zoological Society Collection*)

Richard Montano receives much deserved recognition for his work from Jonnie McFarland and Carol Rickman. He built the shipwrecked *Thatcher*, designed the animal habitats and oversaw their construction, restored the drinking fountain, the historic bas-relief, the seal sculpture, the lighthouse, the *Ada Mae*, and five outdoor animal sculptures. In retrospect it is almost unbelievable that he did so very much to make the Islands of Life possible.

(*Image courtesy of Tammy Guarienti, Pueblo Zoological Society Collection*)

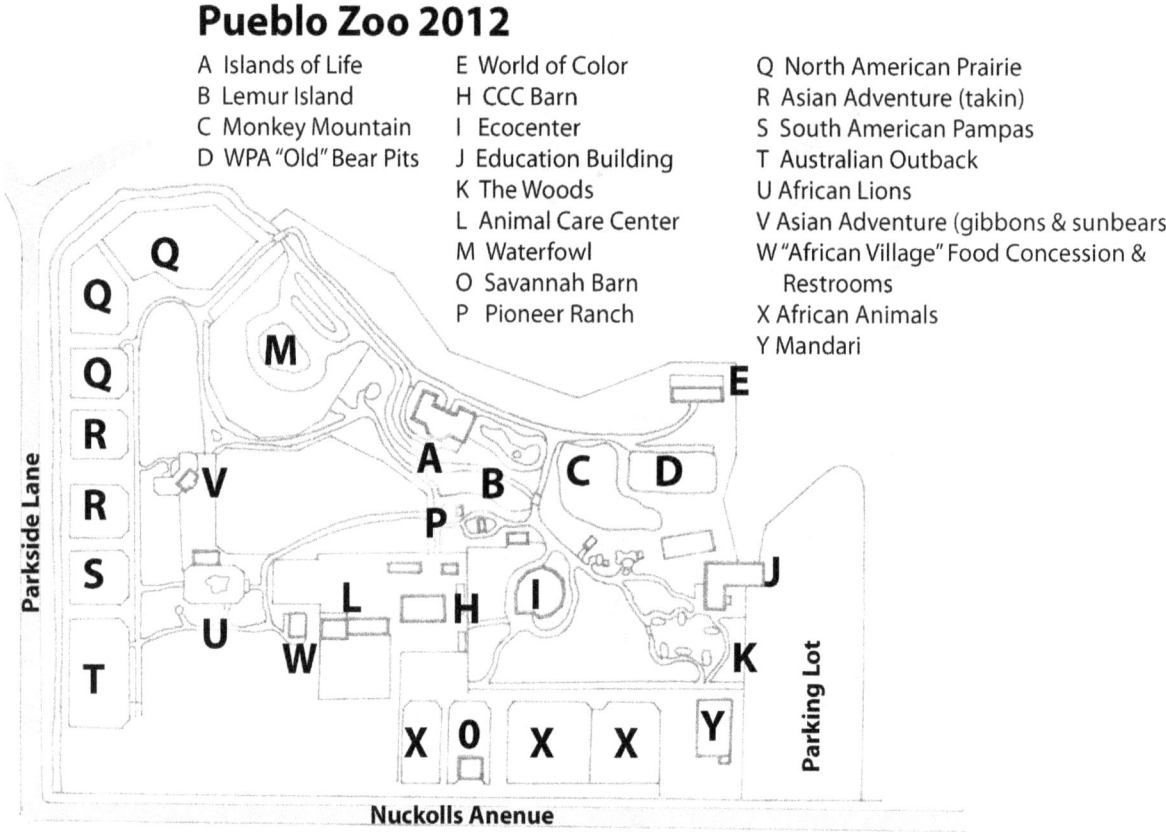

Map of the Pueblo Zoo, 2012.

(*Drawing by Richard Montano, Legend by Steven McDonald*)

Chapter Five

Bringing Learning to Life

*In the end we will conserve only what we love;
we will love only what we understand;
and we will understand only what we are taught.*[1]

Soon after the Pueblo Zoological Society was formed in 1976, and long before it assumed management of the Pueblo Zoo in 1991, those involved with the organization concluded that the only justification for keeping animals in captivity was if they were used as ambassadors for their species. As a result, the Society made the creation of a wildlife education program one of its highest priorities. Most of the Zoo's education offerings were initiated during the 1970s and 1980s, with improvement and expansion during the ensuing decades.

The Pueblo Zoo Education Program Through the Years

Marti Osborn, a certified teacher, was a natural to create the new program. She first met with Bill Aragon, General Curator and Educator at the Cheyenne Mountain Zoo, to learn about programming and the use of docents. She then worked with a committee to develop a thirty-hour docent-training program and a four-part curriculum at the fourth-grade level. Outreach presentations on reptiles, birds, and mammals were followed by a guided tour of the Zoo.

As the education program was being developed, a core group of volunteers was being recruited for program presentation. These were the first Zoo Docents—Karen Adams, Judy Alsever, Sondra Biddle, Carol Chimento, and Laura Mattoon, the same women who had painted the Animal House cages. Docents became essential to the success of the Zoo's education program.

Society member Sylvia Lane's fourth-grade class at Highland Park Elementary School was the first to participate in the new program. Afterwards, Sylvia wrote a letter to the editor of the

---

[1] Senegalese forestry engineer Baba Dioum, speech at the International Union for the Conservation of Nature and Natural Resources, 1968.

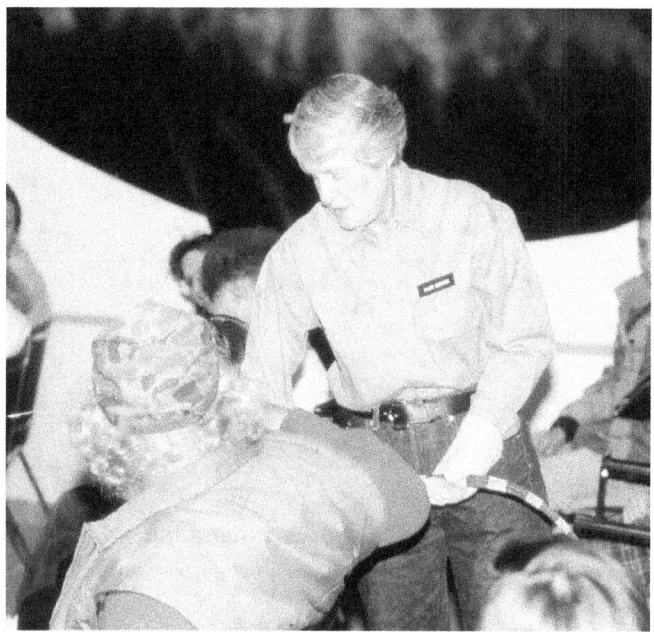

Marti showing a snake to a group in the
Education Building classroom.

(*Image courtesy of the Pueblo Zoological Society*)

Chieftain expressing her opinion about the unique opportunity her students had in seeing live animals and biofacts up close. "As the lessons progressed, we realized the fantastic potential this small zoo holds as an educational resource for all kids from 6 to 60."[2]

Jonnie McFarland, who became a Zoo Docent in 1977, tells her story.

> My introduction to the education program was attendance with four others at a training luncheon, where I was asked to follow along on an upcoming tour of the Zoo. On the day of the tour, there were not enough tour guides, and so Marti said to me, "You lead this group." I had not even walked through the Zoo, there were no signs on the cages or pens, and the outdoor pens were filled with uninspiring hoofstock collection of bison plus five very similar members of the deer family. That tour was quite an initiation to something that would lead me to great challenges and joy for the next 35 years![3]

In 1978, the Society began a collaboration with the Pueblo Junior League, which provided grants for the purchase of materials, while in return the Society offered a placement for their members as docents. A high school docent program was added two years later. Upperclassmen presented programs to elementary level students. Unfortunately, when local high schools began to offer more advanced placement programs, they became reluctant to excuse students from classes, thus bringing this arrangement to an end.

---

[2] "Letter to the Editor – Zoo's Help," *The Pueblo Chieftain*, October 31, 1976.
[3] Personal communication, Jonnene McFarland.

Zoo Docent Sidney Clutter, who was not at all afraid of being spat on by an agitated llama, asked if she could work with those South American animals. General Curator Marilyn McBirney provided training, and Sidney purchased all the necessary gear. She soon had llamas walking with her, which delighted visitors and school groups on tour. Becoming known as the Llama Leaders, others joined, including Chris and Marty Hinz, Jack Palmer, and Carol Rickman. The Llama Leaders have faithfully worked with the animals weekly since 1979 and are willing to hold them for shearing, hoof trimming, and veterinary check-ups.

The education program's first out-of-town request came from the elementary school in Sanford, located in the San Luis Valley south of Alamosa, Colorado. Because our education animal collection was quite small, we asked the City zookeepers if we could take the kinkajou, a tropical racoon relative from Central and South America. It had seemed tame enough, when we viewed it in the Animal House. We should have known better, but we didn't stop and think that kinkajous are nocturnal. The animals and the two of us stayed in Alamosa the night before so we could begin presentations early the next morning. In the middle of the night the kinkajou began doing non-stop back flips in its cage, over and over and over. We put the cage in the bathtub, closed the door, and held our ears. At Sanford, class after class saw, touched, and learned about the critters. After the last bell, the cafeteria workers appeared, asking if we would show them the animals, too. Our first out-of-town experience had been very successful, and there would be more to come.

The number of requests for outreach programs grew, and it became obvious that a good-sized vehicle was needed to transport audio-visual equipment, biofacts, and small animals to local schools and on road trips to surrounding communities. Jonnie's mother, Irene Dunlop, a phone company retiree, asked the company to donate a used van to the Society. We lined the metal floor with donated carpet, and the City adorned its sides with the Society logo and the van's new name—Zoomobile.

Another memorable road trip was to the Lamar Elementary School, located about 110 miles east of Pueblo. Again, we thought we needed to include a more exotic animal. The City zookeepers were raising a young bobcat, kept in a cage in the old "meat house" but often let out to roam inside the building. After we arrived in Lamar, we began to worry when the young bobcat would touch neither food nor water. A call to the Senior Zookeeper resulted in a recommendation to make sure it had water, but no explanation of the problem. At the end of the long day of programs, Marti stayed in the gym to pack up while Jonnie carried the bobcat's cage and a bowl of water to the Zoomobile. The heavy metal door closed behind her as she exited the gym. School had let out, the children had gone home, and there was no one in sight. She put the cage into the Zoomobile, leaving the sliding door wide open as she opened the cage and put in the water. The bobcat immediately grabbed her arm with his strong, claw-armed paws and buried his head with open mouth in the palm of her hand. She was alone, and the door to the gym was impervious to her shouts. All she could think was that the bobcat would bite down hard, she would be forced to let go, and the animal would be on its way to Kansas with the two of us in BIG trouble. After what seemed like 5 minutes of terror, Marti emerged from the building and came to her rescue. On arriving back at the Zoo, the animal was taken for an x-ray, which revealed that it had swallowed the end of a baby bottle nipple, what seemed to it to be a tasty treat. Surgery extracted the nipple, and the cat healed successfully.

Understandably, finding funds to operate the education program always was a challenge. In the 1980s, School District #60 Science Coordinator Sam Genova received a federal grant that included funding for the Zoo to develop and present programs for all 1st, 2nd, and 4th grade classes in the District. The grant terminated at the end of 10 years, after which Marti worked with the administrations of both local school districts to secure on-going annual allocations that continued well beyond her retirement.

Marti tried everything she could think of to let teachers know that the Zoo had programs that could enhance the required curriculum. She went to principals' and teachers' meetings, wrote letters to schools, invited teachers to coffees at the Zoo, taught college summer classes on utilizing the Zoo, and participated in Teaching Environmental Science Naturally (TEN). A cooperative venture with Colorado Parks and Wildlife that began in 1992, each summer TEN offered teachers a week-long continuing education course that included both pre-designed curricula and suggested resource-site activities. The program gave teachers many outdoor experiences at various locations, including the Zoo, where they camped overnight.

In 1985, the Society began to offer educational day camps for elementary age children. Though it started with volunteer teachers, in later years contract teachers led the camps with volunteers assisting. Camps always had interesting themes, such as *Penguins and Their Feathered Friends*, *What Makes Our Zoo Tick?*, or *No Legs, 2 Legs, 4 Legs*. The kids loved watching a race run by numbered Madagascar hissing cockroaches.

Campers study a tiger skull shown by Education Assistant Mary Tucey, one of several professional teachers, including Kathleen Rogers, Sue Alberico, and Donna Stevens.

(*Image courtesy of Pueblo Zoological Society*)

Teacher Christi Osborn Kurtz introduces campers to a snake.

(*Image courtesy of Pueblo Zoological Society*)

Docent Elaine Adley works with a Zoo Quest teen.

(*Image courtesy of Pueblo Zoological Society*)

Docents Jim Edson, Doris McCray, Doris Quinlan, and Edith Edson.

(*Image courtesy of* The Pueblo Chieftain)

Zoo Quest, a summer camp and volunteer experience for middle school teens started in 2009 was a more formal outgrowth of the ZooCrew program that was originated and staffed by General Curator Marilyn McBirney and the zookeepers during the mid-1990s.

Over time, the Zoo Docent group continued to grow and change, but a few remained faithful while we were at the Pueblo Zoo. Some are named in other stories, but there were many, many more—Betty Wheeler, Karen Elliot, Mona Clark, Alberta Tennant, Dolly Koehler, Erma Dempsky, Alice Bunch, Mary Finnan, Jack and Mary Palmer, Ilo Grisham, Marion Guererro, Colleen Ruede, Jane Obaugh, Gwen Francis, Robin Moritz, Mary Beck, Kay Stillman, Carol Ann Moore-Ede, Orla O'Callahan, and Mona Clark. Of course, memory may fail, and we likely have left out a considerable number of volunteers who made our achievements and those of the Society possible. Whether named here or not, because of these truly dedicated people, hundreds of thousands of students gained an understanding of the animals that share Earth with us.

Many of the Zoo Docents have stories of their own. Driving down the freeway on the way to a school, a snake escaped and disappeared under the seats of Sidney Clutter's car. One docent went to a school to do a program and ended up in the wrong classroom at the wrong school, but gave the program anyway. Several times docents were assigned to lead scheduled tours, but mistakenly led groups of regular visitors.

Through the years, we tried many things to recruit new docents and to keep those we had. Monthly luncheons with guest speakers were important, as were field trips to places like the

Denver Zoo or Mission Wolf in Westcliffe, Colorado. Although not very good at counting hours for each docent, we did hold a recognition luncheon where annual pins were awarded. As Marti says, "We laughed, we sang, and sometimes acted very silly, but we always had a great time together. I truly believe these things helped build the camaraderie that kept docents coming back!"

Adult and Family Education

The Zoo offered internships, which included ones in education through the Biology Department of what was then the University of Southern Colorado (now Colorado State University—Pueblo), in zookeeping through Pikes Peak Community College (Colorado Springs), and in veterinary technology through from Pima Medical Institute (Denver).

In 1998, the Zoo began to involve senior mechanical engineering technology students from USC in projects that would provide valuable experience for them and at the same time be beneficial to the Zoo. The students were responsible for design, construction, installation, and whenever possible, acquiring donated materials for their projects. In the lion holding building the students installed a custom-built squeeze cage between two sets of cages, which allowed the animals to become accustomed to passing through it as they moved between the spaces. Once a lion was in the squeeze cage, both ends could be closed and one side moved closer to the other, immobilizing the animal so that the veterinarian could safely administer an injection or perform a limited examination safely and without anesthesia.

Another USC project was in the Cold-Blooded Creatures building where the basement, used for food storage, was accessed via a steeply inclined ship's ladder. True to its name, the ladder was very difficult to navigate, especially while carrying something bulky or heavy. In 1999, the students invented the "snake-a-vator" that has a 96-inch vertical rise and is powered by an electric winch to safely carry up to 150 pounds. The students' project in 2000 was in the Animal Care Center, where they put in an electrically operated lift for the management of large animals inside the building's high-ceilinged stall.

A USC senior engineering technology student demonstrates the "snake-a-vator."

(*Image courtesy of* The Pueblo Chieftain)

Guest speaker Peter Gros of *Mutual of Omaha's Wild Kingdom*, with (*left to right*) Society Board President Corinne Koehler, Marti Osborn, and Jonnie McFarland in 1993.

(*Image courtesy of the Pueblo Zoological Society*)

In September 1988, the Society held its first annual dinner that combined adult education with fundraising. The first guest was Susan Engfer, Director of the Cheyenne Mountain Zoo. The dinner event continued for several years, featuring such prominent speakers as Director of the National Zoo Michael Robinson, Peter Gros and Jim Fowler from *Mutual of Omaha's Wild Kingdom*, Denver Zoo Executive Director Clayton Freiheit, Founder and Curator of the Butterfly Pavilion at Westminster, Colorado, Dr. Mike Weissmann, and finally Dr. Donna Fernandes, at the time Associate Curator at Prospect Park Wildlife Center in Brooklyn, New York. Dr. Fernandes visited close to Valentine's Day, and her topic was "Sex in the Zoo." There was much giggling when she had audience members pin a certain private male part on various insects and other animals … but … the last animal was a human! Some of the guests were more than a little upset and rather vocal in their complaints.

One way to reach all ages was the monthly "Creature Feature" published in *The Pueblo Chieftain*. Soon after the Society assumed management of the Zoo, the feature editor asked that a docent write a monthly article about one of the animals. Milt Kanzaki was the first to volunteer, and he continued to write the articles for many years. He searched the literature and interviewed Zoo staff to gather behind-the-scenes information. A photographer from the paper captured a photograph. After Milt retired, Alex Laput took on the job until Tom Galusha assumed the role in March 2006, writing faithfully until 2012.

Sometimes education took over the entire Zoo. Dinosaur Day in 2001 brought together the University of Colorado Science Outreach, the Denver Museum of Nature and Science, and the Canon

Docent Joe Duran shows one of many Zoo turtles and tortoises during the ever-popular Turtle Tuesday.

(*Image courtesy of Pueblo Zoological Society*)

City's Dinosaur Depot. In 2002, Wolf Awareness Week featured Yellowstone National Park Ranger Bill Wengeler, Nez Perce storyteller Levi Holt, and representatives of Mission Wolf.[4]

Other Aspects of Zoo Education

Zoo education has many facets, including the production of interpretive signs and graphics. In 1976, there was only one sign at any animal exhibit. The WPA had carved "African Lion" into a piece of wood decades earlier. Early on, the Society placed rather primitive (paper glued to pieces of stained plywood) signs on the Animal House cages. From there the signs progressed from ones that involved a photographic process that printed them on metal to full-color ones made by a local sign company.

Very early in the Society's life, the two authors met with City Planner Chris Burkhart about making a map of the Zoo. He suggested they contact local artist Richard Montano. Because Richard produced such an excellent map, the Society contracted with him to design the Zoo's first interpretive graphic display, one on reptiles that was first placed at the wall of snake and lizard exhibits in the Animal House and later moved to the Cold-Blooded Creatures building.

Interpretive graphics would be installed throughout the Zoo in the following years. They gave visitors the opportunity to learn a wide variety of information about habitats and cultures, as well

---

[4] During the event Levi Holt helped dedicate the tipi that Juan Espinosa helped erect near the North American exhibit in Grasslands of the World.

On the Pueblo Zoo's first interpretive graphic the lettering and illustrations were hand-painted by Richard Montano.

(*Image courtesy of Pueblo Zoological Society*)

as about the species they were viewing. During our tenure, almost all of them were researched and designed in-house.

One of the best ways to reach people with a wildlife education message is by letting them see and touch real biofacts, such as live mounts, skins, feather, or skulls. When the education program began, it had only a couple of skins and a live mounted armadillo. But when opportunity knocked, we learned how to take advantage of it. The words "road kill" may conjure up visions of some hairy or feathery critter flattened on the road, but it was not always so to the two of us. We picked them up, put them in plastic bags, and took them home where we traumatized our families with DIY taxidermy. Although preparing dead animals for use in education programs was not much fun, it was necessary because of how important it is for people to be able to touch and explore things. Better learning takes place when more senses are involved. We began collecting road kill and parts from deceased Zoo animals in 1977 and continued to hold USFWS and Colorado Parks and Wildlife salvage permits until we retired. We personally prepared many biofacts over the years, but sometimes resorted to taxidermists for larger skins, skulls, or live mounts. From time to time, we accepted the donation of mounted specimens, though some were not in prime condition. The collection included a beautiful but ill-prepared mute swan that dripped grease, a coyote with very little hair on its tail, and a skunk with an extremely pointed nose.

We learned how to prepare birds in an ornithology class. For mammals, we spent many hours observing a real taxidermist. Carcasses had to be skinned, which required a very sharp knife and

In 1979, 4th-graders Kelton Osborn and
Janet McFarland Burlile examine biofacts.

(*Image courtesy of Pueblo Zoological Society*)

the courage to slip your hand under the skin to loosen it from the flesh. If we wanted only the skull, we had to remove the brain from the inside and the muscles from the outside. We will not describe that process! One evening Marti was boiling a small skull on her stove at home. One of her son's friends smelled what he thought was soup and snuck a taste—quite a surprise! To make an avian study skin to give children a general idea of what a certain bird looked like, we carefully skinned the bird, and then stuffed it with cotton and placed a stick through an opening in the lower abdomen. Zoo Docents called them "bird-sicles."

In 1986, after we had moved into the Education Building and were developing the Discovery Room, Marti was preparing the partial skull of a walrus, a confiscated item that we received on loan from US Fish and Wildlife Service. Evidently, to collect the ivory of a walrus, the front of its skull is removed, skinned, and dried. We had to boil the piece of skull to remove the stinky, dried flesh, so Marti put it on the stove in the education animal kitchen in a huge pot with its long tusks sticking out. The smell was overwhelming. One of the Parks Department employees had been checking on our progress with Discovery Room displays each and every day, much in doubt that we would ever get the room finished and opened. When he came in that morning, he asked what in the world smelled so bad. We showed him. He left and never returned to check on us. No doubt he thought we had gone over the edge!

We always were on the lookout for specimens we could use in programs or displays. We found a dried-out vole in a mountain cabin bathtub. We had a shrew shipped from West Virginia. We were lucky to acquire several collections of butterflies and other arthropods. Judy Bertholf, daughter of docent JoAnn, gave us the collection she had gathered for her Ph.D. in entomology. Dr. Jay Linam, University of Southern Colorado biology professor, was always willing to help us identify various

Nicole and Brooke Guarienti look at the arthropod display in the Discovery Room. In the center is a collection of Colorado butterflies donated by Dr. Maurice Howard, University of Southern Colorado psychology professor.

(*Image courtesy of Rick Avalos Photography, Pueblo Zoological Society collection*)

arthropods and generously gave us many specimens. Local physician Dr. Anthony Ortegon donated beautiful tropical insect specimens that he had collected in Colombia.

We did not stop with arthropod collections, however. Dr. Fred Shaeffer, a University of Southern Colorado geology professor, donated a collection of fossils, many of which we used in a display of extinct and endangered animals in the Discovery Room. Rosemount Museum, as well as several zoos from around the country, gave us bird eggshells for a Discovery Room display about birds. Seashells collected by Elsie McFarland were displayed in the Discovery Room ocean display. It quite literally took an act of Congress to import whale vertebra from an acquaintance in Bermuda, and a sailor sent us a desiccated giant hermit crab from Johnston Atoll in the Pacific.

Marti's vision was helping people of all ages discover the wonders of life on Earth, to learn to appreciate and respect all aspects of the living world, and hopefully, to translate these attitudes into lifestyles that would support a sustainable future and the votes needed to improve the future of Earth's creatures. Although we both are very proud of our accomplishments in providing quality educational opportunities for so many, we know it could not have been possible without the help and dedication of so many wonderful people—docents, staff, volunteers, and an entire community that accepted and encouraged us all along the way!

Chapter Six

Fun, Friends, and Fundraising

When it came to raising money for Zoo operation and improvements, the Zoological Society left no stone unturned. There were grant proposals; frequent mailings; requests for in-kind donations; sponsorships and underwriters for events, benches, trees, and even trash cans; a car donation program; rentals for weddings, picnics, birthday parties, and meetings; gift and food sales; penny pressing machines; a pay phone; and fundraising parties. Membership was important from the beginning but moved to a new level after the Society assumed management of the Zoo, when free admission could be offered as a valuable perk. We started a newsletter, a website, a Facebook page, and we launched six capital campaigns, completing five of them by the time we retired.[1] Of the many events the Society held over the years, some did not survive, some were intended to be short-lived, some burned out after a few years, but a special few became community traditions.

Special Events and Fund-raising Activities

Special events are held to increase visitation, build community support, educate the public, and secondarily, to produce revenue. In contrast, ones that have income production as their primary goal are considered to be fund-raising activities. They often have minimal relationship to the mission of an organization and may be held off-site.[2]

Selling beer at a 1980s airshow was the Zoological Society's first fund-raising activity to benefit the Zoo. It sounded like a winner in September. The Parks Department set up a booth at the airport and helped stock it with plenty of beer and ice. But typical Colorado weather sent us a snowstorm instead of two hot days. The two of us, a few hardy volunteers, and one of the City zookeepers spent

---

[1] ZOONEWS, the Zoological Society's newsletter, was started in 1977. The first editor was Margaret Crader. The second editor was Helen Trent, a journalist retired from *The Pueblo Chieftain*. When she no longer wished to do the work, Zoo staff took it on.

[2] Jonnene McFarland, "The Impact of Diversified Activities on the Revenue Structures of Nonprofit Zoological Parks in the United States," Unpublished Report on Directed Research for MBA, Department of Business Administration, University of Southern Colorado, 1988.

a miserable weekend in the booth trying our best to convince folks to buy our ice-cold beer. We should have sold coffee and hot chocolate! Who knew!

ZooRun, sponsored by the Society beginning in 1982, was an annual cross-country run through City Park and down the nine-hole golf course. A joint effort with the Southern Colorado Runners Club, it was planned by a very small committee, headed by Jan Pullaro and Carolyn Lowrey. Meetings were held at the Gold Dust Saloon on Union Avenue where the four of us enjoyed their famous chocolate cake with lunch. Very successful for a number of years, the run's popularity and profits waned as similar events became available to the area's running public.

Feast with Father, a 1980s special event, was an outdoor Father's Day pancake breakfast. It was both lots of work and lots of fun. It lasted just long enough for all of the necessary pancake-making equipment to be acquired. Once revenues did not justify the expenses, there were no more pancakes. Our professional pancake plopper was passed on to others, and the event morphed into free admission for fathers, mothers, and grandparents on their special days. An outstanding memory was thawing pre-mixed scrambled eggs (mistakenly put into the walk-in freezer) with docent Virginia Smith in the Education Building animal room (yes, live animals in cages), using a blow dryer, while praying that the health department would not appear.

Senior Safari continues beyond the writing of this book as one of the most heart-warming Zoo special events. Beginning in 1993, residents of senior facilities and other old timers are invited to a special day in September where they can enjoy tours, animals close-up, pizza, bingo, and music. The parking lot is still regularly jammed with vans and buses from communities across Southeastern Colorado. Free admission for those aged 65 and older continues during the rest of Senior Week.

Zoopalz and their Valentine's Day parties were the idea of Louise Keach. She recruited Patty Bedard, and in 2003 they founded an auxiliary with the single mission of holding an annual Valentine's Day party to raise funds to support the Zoo. This group of about twenty women found spectacular homes for party sites, made guest lists, sent invitations, handled mailings, and accepted RSVPs. They made special hors d'oeuvres, fancy desserts, and other yummy edibles, as well as donating champagne, wine, and beer. Red decorations, together with members of Zoopalz and many of their guests dressed in red, turned each party into a Valentine vision. These lovely events continued for eleven years, raising many thousands of dollars for Zoo projects and operations.

The Spring Plant Sale was instituted in 2006 by Marti Osborn, who was joined in 2009 by the Master Gardeners and Linda McMulkin, the Horticulture Coordinator for the Colorado State University Extension Service in Pueblo. One of the challenges in holding an outdoor plant sale in early May was the weather. One year a freeze was predicted after thousands of dollars in plants had been delivered to the Mandari. The hasty rental of propane heaters saved the plants during the night, while hot chocolate and donuts did the same for volunteers the next morning. This event proved to be such a good educational and financial collaboration, it continued for many years until both Linda and Marti retired.

The *ZooPalz* ladies are ready for their 2009 party.
(*Image courtesy of Patty Bedard*)

Some events came and went, including the Teddy Bear Picnic, Fall Festival, and several iterations of an Earth Day celebration. A free day held on the 4th of July resulted in five thousand visitors, rocks thrown at animals, vandalism, and lots of trash. Wine tasting parties were discontinued due to liability and security concerns. ZooBoo lasted for a few years, was ended by the blizzard of 1997, and then several years later was successfully revived. Family campouts held in the Zoo proved to be very popular.

Zoofari

Zoofari was the longest running Zoological Society fundraising activity. This outdoor dinner held each June started so long ago that no one seems to be sure of the exact year, although it had to be sometime in the 1980s. Early ones were held in rented tents set up just to the south of the birdcages (future Woods). One year it rained very hard before the guests were to arrive. Rainwater sheeted off the top of the tent and down the sides, drenching the grass underneath and forming large pools. Marti scouted out large pieces of cardboard to line areas between the tables, hoping to prevent high heels from sinking deep into the soggy sod. Chairman Laura Mattoon and Jonnie used broom handles to poke the top of the tent, pushing off huge volumes of water.

Beginning in 1986, Zoofari tents often were positioned on the west side of the new Education Building. Rain played a role in one of them, too. Just as dinner was ending, it began to rain so hard that all of the guests were trapped inside the tent. No one could sneak out to avoid the auction, which yielded more than ever before.

At the Raiders of the Lost Ark Zoofari, Cathy Spangler, Tom Compton, Bill Mattoon, and Wanda the camel pose for a Sandy Stein *Social Seasonings* column photo.

(*Image courtesy of* The Pueblo Chieftain)

Marilyn McBirney and Ronna Paterson pose with Wanda at the 1993 Zoofari.

(*Image courtesy of the McBirney Family*)

Richard Montano generally created the logo for each Zoofari. His rough sketch for the 1998 Zoofari invitation looks a lot like Dr. Zoolittle (Dr. Mark Rickman) and his assistant Carol with llama Arika.

(*Images courtesy of the Pueblo Zoological Society*)

Sidney Clutter, John Wark, JoAnn Bertholf, and Bill Brill at "Come Grow with Us" Zoofari in 1997.

(*Image courtesy of* The Pueblo Chieftain)

Cathy Spangler followed Laura Mattoon as event chair, coming up with very creative themes and ideas. One of them, a Medieval-themed event, was a pig roast. Cathy arranged for some experts to roast a whole pig at the Zoo. The lengthy process started the evening before the event, keeping Marketing and Events Coordinator Pat Ponce up all night with the chefs.

In 1991, Sally Mara joined the Zoofari "Party Animals," the volunteers in charge of decorations. Carol Rickman came on board a year or so later, and it was not long until the two of them assumed leadership of the whole event. This pair soon became infamous for bringing even more rain to the Zoofari, often credited with breaking months-long droughts. For many years, Marilyn's mother Ronna Paterson addressed the invitations and wrote all of the bid sheets with her beautiful calligraphy, Sandy Stein featured every Zoofari in her *Social Seasonings* society column, and Danny Masterson developed seating charts. In 1997 the Mandari group picnic shelter became the permanent home of Zoofari.

Over the years, Sally and Carol came up with many themes: Animal Ark; Climb High featuring tours of Monkey Mountain with champagne toasts at the summit; Island Adventure in 2001; Take a Ride on the Wild Side in 2005 offering guests a ride in the local utility company's bucket truck; The Wild West; Fiesta Olé Otters in 2003; Passport to Adventure in 2008; Wings of the World in 2009; Treasure the Endangered in 2011; and the one in 2012 (our final involvement) Celebrating the Past, Present, and Future. There was always entertainment: Chinese dragon dancers, African drummers, David Traylor's "Rainforest," the Fireweed bluegrass band, cowgirl poet Maggie Mae Sharp, and hissing cockroach races. Alan Polivka and his band were so popular that they were invited to play year after year. One of the most unusual activities was placing a bet on the square where a hedgehog might poop.

Zoofari always included money-raising activities. Silent and live auctions were common, but other forms of money-raising were also used, such as selling keys for a chance to open a small chest full of gift cards, with only one of those keys being a winner. Experiential prizes were often the best sellers. Bidders loved opportunities to be a zookeeper for a day, to travel with the Pueblo SWAT team, or to have a gourmet dinner in the penguin viewing area. When Krispy Kreme Doughnuts first came to Colorado, Mike Blazer brought a fresh dozen from Denver, and those twelve donuts started a bidding war, selling for $150!

Guided tours of the Zoo were part of the Zoofari program, but often proved an uncomfortable hike for dolled-up guests. In 1992, some of the attendees decided there needed to be a new way to tour. Reg Landrum and Chuck Hedrick donated a used truck. Mike Stillman paid for needed repairs and installation of seats, railings, and steps into the bed, while Kay Stillman painted the vehicle with zebra stripes. It fondly became known as the Zoofari Truck. Keeping it clean and in condition for tours was a challenge readily accepted by Reg and his friend Bill Crane. Sometimes the truck was covered, sometimes stored in a volunteer's garage, and finally kept in the City's downtown parking garage where the police cars were parked.

ElectriCritters

ElectriCritters was the result of our visit in 1992 to the Phoenix Zoo's spectacular holiday light show Zoolights. It was the first show of its kind either of us had seen, although there were some at other zoos. That same year, the Colorado State Fair decided to end their drive-through holiday light event, providing a great opening for the Zoo.

In the fall of 1993, Marketing and Events Coordinator Pat Ponce took on our challenge to develop what would be called ElectriCritters. She best tells the story.

> I had never seen such a display, but Marti and Jonnie had. They told me what they knew, and I called several zoos around the country. I got the best help from Folsom's Children's Zoo in Lincoln, Nebraska, while the Denver Zoo warned us not to offer free admission, as the public would expect it from then on.
>
> Our "mission" was to provide a different look at animals as part of the holiday events available in town and to begin building a moneymaking event during the sparse winter season. Animals eat in winter, too.
>
> Because the Zoo could afford only a few lighted displays and had very little available electricity, I decided to develop as rich a lighting display as possible along the straight sidewalk that ran from the Education Building to the Ecocenter. By talking to electrician Larry Moore, I learned all kinds of new concepts, such as amps and watts and how much electricity it takes to run so many strings of lights. And, with the help of the local electric utility, we were able to take lighting 20 to 30 feet above the sidewalk. Their Operations Manager, Brett Opfer, provided a smaller bucket truck along with two kind, but tough, linemen. As we were placing some lights in trees surrounding the electrified rhinoceros, I explained that I wanted blue and white mini-light strings placed in the trees. "Tell them to arrange the lights to look like fluffy white clouds in a lovely blue sky," I said. Brett turned to me in horror and said, "I'm not going to say that! You tell them!"
>
> Richard Montano designed and built frames for the lighted displays—a 12-foot tall logo, elephant with calf, giraffe, orangutan, and rhinoceros. He also built lighted fiberglass sculptures of a penguin pair and a chick, and we purchased two lighted deer. Richard attached rope lights to the logo sign, as we only had enough money for rope light for one critter. The grounds guys, some volunteers, and I wrapped mini-light strings around all the others.
>
> During the event, docents offered animal encounters in all four buildings. The rainforest was closed; the penguin exhibit was open. Members of the Board of Directors were stationed along the sidewalks with flashlights for public safety, and a caterer offered hot drinks and simple snacks from his serving trailer. Holiday music was broadcast via two loud speakers from the Ecocenter animal kitchen. Before each night's opening, grounds workers Dave Korber and Brian Spangler would run from display to display with me, plugging in cords. Then, at closing time, we would reverse the process.
>
> Because much of the display could be seen through the chain-link fence between the grounds and the parking lot, some sort of screening was needed. But, of course, there was no money to buy it. JoAnne and John Bertholf came to our rescue by donating many large plastic covered paper sheets, used to cover wood trusses manufactured by their company. These were attached to the fencing, and then the winds came. They blew hard every day, ripping off the sheets, one by one. Day after day, a few Useful Public Service "volunteers" and I would re-attach them. In the end, I won! The show was successfully screened from viewing without paying $1 at the gate. And, even better—my no-nonsense sister declared, "It's magical!"

Faithful volunteers Neil Wainwright, Pablo Ramirez, Lynn Wainwright, and Joan Ramirez in 2010.

(*Image courtesy of* The Pueblo Chieftain)

Docent Anita Bandell hangs origami animals made by Origami Odyssey at the Pueblo Zoo on a tree displayed during ElectriCritters in 1999.

(*Image courtesy of* The Pueblo Chieftain)

ElectriCritters always had a Candy Cane Café, although it moved from early days in the Cold-Blooded Creatures building to the Watering Hole snack bar and finally to the lobby of the Ecocenter. Pictured here in her holiday outfit, Manager Verona Miller asked Board of Directors members to volunteer. After they had done it once, they signed up year after year, thinking it great fun to work for this very-much-in-charge little lady.

(*Image courtesy of the Pueblo Zoological Society*)

Elaine Zavislan assumed the job of managing ElectriCritters after Pat's retirement. Next came Jackie Bernal, who proposed several new schemes and was willing to go the extra mile to make them succeed. In her first year, she wanted to make a big splash on the opening night and so organized a parade of sponsors, media, and invited dignitaries. While the group wound down darkened paths, Jackie waved a wand and as if by magic the lights appeared. The guests had no idea that several staff members were hiding in the dark, plugging in the lights at her radioed command and then running through the darkness to electrify yet another section. Once was enough for this special activity.

The next year, Jackie added a volcano to the show. Her plan involved covering the entire south side of Monkey Mountain with twinkling orange and red lights to simulate flowing, red hot lava. At the summit, smoke was to billow from a theatrical-type fogger. Most of us thought it was an outrageous idea, but under Jackie's direction and with the hard work of the grounds crew, it was spectacular, looking pretty much like a volcano. The public loved it, but once was enough for this one, too.

The same year that she created the volcano, Jackie decided to take advantage of the recent birth of Klaus, a reindeer calf. Because the North American Aerospace Defense Command, headquartered near Colorado Springs, is known for the "official" tracking of Santa Claus on his rounds, she asked them to send Air Force public relations officers to Pueblo to announce that the young reindeer had been chosen to enter flight school to be trained to pull Santa's sleigh!

ElectriCritters turned into a completely homegrown community tradition, continuing far beyond our retirements in 2012. For the first few years, Richard Montano fabricated, designed, and installed the critters. He continued the design and installation, but after a few years, bending and welding the metal rods into creatures was taken over by welding students from Pueblo Community College and industrial arts students from Pueblo County High School. Beginning in 1998, volunteers Lynn and Neil Wainwright with Joan and Pablo Ramirez fastened rope lights on the figures and maintained them throughout each of the events.

Other Ways of Raising Money for the Zoo

Through the years, the Society Board and Zoo staff came up with many other ways to raise money for both operations and capital campaigns. Following are a few of the more unique ones we tried.

One way to raise funds for the Zoo was by selling artwork created by the animals using non-toxic paint and with the assistance of zookeepers. This porcupine was one of the most prolific artists.

(Image courtesy of the Pueblo Zoological Society)

Ol'90 in a ditch before a fence was built
along the west perimeter.

(*Image courtesy of* The Pueblo Chieftain)

ADOPT (Animals Depend On People, Too) began in the late 1970s with the Pueblo Elks Lodge 90's adoption of Ol' 90, a bull elk. At the time, there were 65 animal species in the Zoo, and adoption donations, used to buy animal food, ranged from $15 for a bullfrog to $500 for an African lion.

The Animals' Non-Party was initiated in 1985 and continued for the next 28 Decembers. The Society sent invitations to a party that did not happen. Instead, the invitation asked invitees to stay home and send contributions to help feed and care for the animals. The end-of-the-year campaign proved to be so successful that many donors looked forward to receiving their annual invitation.

INVITATION TO THE 20th ANNUAL NON-PARTY IN 2005

The weather was cold; attendance was down.
"Oh my," said King Lion with a very large frown.

"We have new ones—and old ones—to feed as before.
They're our cubs, pups, and lambkins whom we love more & more."

"Oh, gee," grumped the bear, "Just what can we do?
We work very hard to impress with our Zoo!"

"Now wait!" said the zebra, shaking his mane,
"You forget our Non-Party; it's still the same.

Let's invite all our friends to a stay-at-home feast.
With a grand invitation from each bird and beast.

We'll ask our Zoo friends NOT to come to our fest,
But send us a check and make this one the best!"

(Poem by Betty Wilkinson, graphic by Richard Montano)

Whether successful, sort of successful, or a total bust, each special event or fund-raising activity required much work on the part of employees, willing volunteers, and collaborating organizations. The two of us were personally involved with most of them. Some of them were fun, some were hard, and some were downright discouraging. Through all of them we made new friends while raising the funds needed to operate and improve the Pueblo Zoo.

Chapter Seven

The Animals

When people hear that you work at a zoo, they typically comment on how much fun it must be. Of course, they are right. It is fun. But it is a whole lot more, some of it not so much fun. Both of us developed a love and respect for nature through childhood experiences and were very fortunate to have become involved in the business of exhibiting and interpreting the living world. Working at the Pueblo Zoo brought us face-to-face with real life—the fun, the tragedy, the worry, the joy.

People sometimes feel animals would be better off if they were not confined in zoos and instead allowed to live their lives in their native habitats. In an ideal world that might be possible, but in an ideal world all humans would understand how critical it is to protect our planet and all of its inhabitants. Except for a kangaroo rat and a few arthropods, the Zoo's animals were all captive born, many of whose ancestors had been under human care for generations. We, the authors, came to realize that beyond providing a home for animals, zoos play a crucial role, and we hope our commitment to animal welfare, conservation, and education will inspire others.

This chapter includes stories we heard from the past, as well as ones about the animals we knew. We personally looked after and supervised the care of many of the smaller animals used in education presentations or exhibited in the Discovery Room, but management of the larger ones was left to the expertise of the curator, veterinarian, and zookeepers.

Monkeys and More

Monkeys were among the first animals kept on exhibition in Pueblo, with cages of them reported in three parks before being moved to the City Park Zoo. These likely were capuchins. Macaques and spider monkeys are documented as living in the Animal House during the 1940s. There are stories of a chimpanzee kept in a small, opened-fronted Animal House cage. Fed and tormented by the public, it was given cigarettes and allowed to roam through the service area at the end of a heavy chain. In the Animal House during the 1980s there were De Brazzas monkeys, capuchin monkeys, baboons, and three or four lemurs.

Hamadryas baboon Tyrone arrived at the Zoo sometime in the mid-1970s. Where he came from has been forgotten. He lived alone in one of the 6.5'x 8' Animal House cages and was a fierce looking and acting creature—very territorial. As visitors approached the front of his cage, he would slam his whole body against the glass, while baring his teeth. It was disturbing to those of us who cared about animals, but it was exciting for visitors, who generally did not understand what his actions really meant. As a consequence, the public harassed him.

In 1980, when he was about 5-years-old, the Parks Department found eighteen-month-old Babs as a mate for him. Babs was introduced successfully to Tyrone over a 12-day period, and from their union came a little female, so ugly that she was cute. Unfortunately, Tyrone's behavior only worsened once he had both a mate and a little one to protect from visitors only a few inches from the glass. Eventually, the trio was sent elsewhere. We have no idea where.

Baboons Tyrone and Babs, 1980.

(*Image courtesy of* The Pueblo Chieftain)

The ring-tailed lemur Mamu had lived in one of the interior exhibits in the Animal House since the early 1970s and had become a tremendous favorite of the public. For Islands of Life, Marilyn acquired other ring-tailed lemurs to make up a troop that was allowed outside to enjoy Monkey Island. Mamu would sit on a rock at the edge of the water, vocalizing to visitors. She lived to be the oldest of her species in captivity at that time, dying of a stroke in 2007 at the age of 37 years. Richard Montano memorialized her with a bronze sculpture located near Monkey Island.

In May 2012, just before our retirements, the ring-tailed lemur Star gave birth to baby Nova. Nova was Star's first baby, and as sometimes happens, her mother rejected her. Marilyn and the zookeepers hand-raised the tiny lemur, and then introduced her back into the exhibit with her mother and her grandmother Cosmo. Grandma Cosmo was the one who stepped up, carrying the baby and holding it while zookeepers gave it bottle-feedings. Nova thrived and grew into a beautiful adult lemur.

Baby Nova in 2012.

(*Image by Nikki Emanuel, courtesy of the McBirney Family*)

Big Cats

Two Bengal tigers arrived at the Zoo sometime in the early 1970s. The City offered naming rights for the pair in the local PBS Channel 8 on-the-air auction. Local philanthropist Bob Johnston purchased the right to name the female Doris, after his wife, and the male Mai Tai (perhaps her favorite cocktail?).

The magnificent Mai Tai.

(*Image courtesy of the Pueblo Zoological Society*)

A decade later, while presenting a program at Goodnight Elementary School, the principal interrupted Marti to say she had just heard on the radio that one of the Zoo's tigers had escaped. Back at the Zoo, Marti learned that a zookeeper had forgotten to lock an outside cage door, and Mai Tai had taken the opportunity to have a look around. A man walking his dog near Monkey Mountain was surprised (an understatement) by the tiger, which attacked and slightly injured the dog. In the nick of time, the Senior Zookeeper used a broom to shoo the tiger back into its cage. The dog healed, and a potentially deadly escapade ended without major damage.

When both of the aged tigers were euthanized because of ill health, the Parks Department Director had a taxidermist prepare their skins and skulls for use in the Zoological Society's education program. We were very pleased to receive these valuable specimens from much-loved Zoo residents, who would be honored in death through respectful presentations about their species.

African lions have long been a part of the Pueblo Zoo, seemingly first arriving in the 1930s. Long-time residents of the Aberdeen subdivision tell of hearing roaring a mile or so from the Zoo.

Leo.

(*Image courtesy of the Pueblo Zoological Society*)

One morning in 1985, Marti's friend Joan Wolther called to ask whether she had seen an article in the *Colorado Springs Sun* about a lion in a cage in the back of a pickup truck.[1] The truck with its wild cargo had been spotted parked at a Colorado Springs motel and reported to the local police. The lion was Leo from the Pueblo Zoo and on his way to the Windy Hill Exotic Animal Farm in Loop City, Nebraska. Leo was part of a three-way deal in which the Zoo received snow leopards Llasa and Wilhelmina from the Cheyenne Mountain Zoo. After several articles about the incident appeared in *The Pueblo Chieftain*, citizen Melvin Collins presented a petition with 250 signatures to City Council. It demanded that the Society, the Council, and citizens approve future animal trades or sales. This surprise move of a major Zoo animal resulted in the Council adopting a policy that gave the Society authority to approve any future animal acquisitions or dispositions. Both Collins and Zoological Society President Linda Stefanic expressed their satisfaction with the new policy.[2]

[1] 1985, clipping in *Pueblo Zoo Album 1976-1987*, Pueblo City-County Library.
[2] "Policy to Cover the Trading of Zoo Animals," *The Pueblo Chieftain*, July 24, 1985.

When the Society assumed management of the Zoo in 1991, the snow leopards Llasa and Wilhelmina still resided in the Animal House. They occupied one of the larger enclosures that had access to an outdoor barred cage, a very sterile environment of just concrete, glass, and bars. There was little for the animals to do other than pace and wait to be fed. After Marilyn McBirney became General Curator, Llasa was sent to another zoo. Then our brand new zookeepers set to work furnishing Wilhelmina's cage with wood mulch, leaves, branches, and logs. When they were finished, they called and asked that Jonnie come to take a look. She could hardly believe her eyes. The zookeepers said that as soon as Wilhelmina was returned to her newly furnished cage, she rolled and played in the mulch and leaves. By the time Jonnie arrived, Wilhelmina was curled up like a princess on a feather mattress, sound asleep. She knew immediately that we had chosen the right young professionals to care for the precious lives with which we were entrusted. A few years later Wilhelmina died at the Zoo of natural causes.

Early in 1992, a woman who had purchased a lion cub at an out-of-state exotic animal auction contacted Marilyn. The animal had grown so large that it could no longer live inside her home in Breckenridge, and winters there were too cold to keep it outdoors. Called Bo, she still had her teeth and claws, a necessity for self-defense if she were to be introduced to others of her kind. We did not want to accept a lioness with no background because she would never be allowed to have cubs under Species Survival Plan (SSP) guidelines. We also did not like the idea of putting another big cat into one of the Animal House exhibits. We decided to accept her, however, as the "poster girl" for a 1992 capital campaign to build a new, modern lion exhibit.

While Bo lived in the Animal House and the Society conducted the capital campaign, she became a favorite not only of visitors, but also of staff, docents, and Board members. Docent and Board member Art Schwager fell for her, and she for him. If he came anywhere near, she recognized him and would start rubbing against the cage bars. Zoo cashier Nancy Lamas often took a long-handled duster and waved it in front of Bo, who seemed to enjoy the play. We did not know anything about this game until Nancy confessed that she had gotten so close that the lion had snatched her duster, and now she was forced to ask for a new one.

Bo in the new lion exhibit, relaxing atop a simulated kopje rock created by Richard Montano.

(*Image courtesy of the McBirney Family*)

In late 1994, Marilyn obtained another lion and lioness, Haya and Yatima. Each got along with Bo separately, but the hope was to exhibit the three cats together. The day came when they were to be let into the outside exhibit together for the first time. Zookeepers were ready with fire extinguishers and hoses in case there was trouble. The rest of the staff was watching at a distance outside the exhibit fence. Bo was the first one let into the exhibit. Haya and Yatima waited inside the holding building. When the pair was released, it was almost as if they had made a plan. They pursued Bo with a vengeance, one running toward her from one side of the kopje; the other, around the other side. The roaring was intense, so loud that it was nearly heart stopping. Lion Section Keeper Heather Smith reacted instantly. As Bo made a beeline for the building, Heather quickly raised the door, and then just as quickly lowered it behind the fleeing animal, no doubt saving the life of the lioness. Needless to say, that was never tried again. Zookeepers continued to rotate two lions at a time on exhibit until Bo's death on January 3, 2003. Her ashes were scattered around the perimeter of the lion exhibit, and a plaque was installed in her memory.

Haya also died in 2003, Yatima in 2007 at the age of 19. In 2005, the Zoo acquired two more lionesses, Ulana and Saida, both born at the Cheyenne Mountain Zoo. They were introduced without incident to a new male received in early 2006, four-year-old Taz Jahari.

From left to right: Ulana, Saida, and Taz Jahari.

(*Image courtesy of the Pueblo Zoological Society*)

On October 5, 2006, Ulana gave birth to two cubs. A month later on November 3, Saida had a single cub. These were the first born at the Zoo since the 1940s, when zookeeper T. P. Hamilton raised cubs. Neither of the females bonded with her offspring, and so the cubs were separated and cared for around-the-clock by four experienced zookeepers along with Marilyn and veterinarian Dr. Kathy Wolyn. Jonnie was allowed the once-in-a-lifetime opportunity to keep all three cubs at home for one night.

Names for the cubs were chosen from over 500 entered from across the country in a naming contest sponsored by the Pueblo Chieftain. The females became Shetani and Jasira, while the male was named Bakari. Upon recommendations from the African Lion Species Survival Plan committee, at about a year of age the cubs were moved to other zoos: Shetani to Springfield, Missouri; Jasira to Minot, North Dakota; and Bakari to Little Rock, Arkansas.

Lion Section Keeper Heather Smith feeding the cubs inside the lion exhibit.

(*Image courtesy of the Pueblo Zoological Society*)

From left to right: Shetani, Jasira, and Bakari at almost one year old.

(*Image courtesy of the Pueblo Zoological Society*)

Little Bears, Big Bears

The Zoo housed eight bears in 1971, one of which was Bruno, a European brown bear, obtained when full-grown from a Kansas animal trader in the early 1960s. According to Head Zookeeper Bill Fritzel in a *Pueblo Chieftain* interview, "He lets you know to stay away. If he got hold of your arm he'd probably tear it off." Bill continued, "Danger signs warn the public to keep clear of a restricted area at the rear of the bear cages, since a clawed paw can swoop swiftly through the bars to reach anyone too close and unwary. The signs sometimes are ignored and, occasionally over the years, blood splotches have been found, indicating that Bruno was a little quicker than a visitor."

Malayan sun bear Solar Sue arrived at the Zoo in 1976 as a youngster. One day she apparently decided to test her climbing skills, escaping from her home in the New Bear Pits. The zookeepers found her walking along Pueblo Boulevard, a busy highway just to the west of the Zoo. They lured her into an animal crate, upon which she inflicted considerable damage. Although weighing only 150 pounds, she was all muscle and armed with long, curved claws. Parks Department workers covered her pit with welded wire, and in 1986 she was moved into a larger outdoor cage built especially for her.

Solar Sue attempted another escape, this time in 1995. After the last big cat was moved out of the cages on the south side of the Animal House, the zookeepers prepared one of them as a comfortable indoor home for the aging bear. After moving her in, they watched while she explored her new surroundings, all seeming fine when they left for the night. Next morning, Sue was high in the attic of the building. She had managed to climb out of the cage, and then claw her way through one of the sides of the cupola, much like she would do if she were tearing open a bees' nest in her native habitat. Sadly, since she couldn't be confined in that cage, it was the end of her new indoor home, and she was moved back to the outdoor enclosure.

In 1998, Sue was moved again, this time to an even more spacious outdoor cage in the new Asian Adventure exhibit, where in 2000 she would meet another of her kind—the large male, Barney. Five years later, she would have two root canals and multiple extractions, which despite her advanced age, she handled very well. In failing health, Solar Sue was euthanized on August 27, 2010 at the very old sun bear age of 33 years.

Solar Sue in her spacious Asian Adventure enclosure.

(*Image courtesty of the McBirney Family*)

One of the most well-known residents of the Old Bear Pits was a polar bear named Al. He was a wonderful old guy who had suffered a gunshot wound many years before in his native Scandinavia. Lame in one of his front paws, he lived in the pit nearest Monkey Mountain, where he had a large pool, part of which was spanned by a short stone bridge. In 1978, there was a commercial on TV in which a fellow drank a glass of Nestea iced tea and found it as refreshing as falling backwards into a pool of cold water. Al perfected the "Nestea plunge," falling backwards from the bridge into the pool, over and over and over again, making a huge splash as he hit the water. He would even wave his crippled paw as he fell backwards. Just about everyone in Pueblo knew and loved Al.

Al the polar bear in the Old Bear Pits pool.
(*Image courtesy of the Pueblo Zoological Society*)

Water for the pools in the Old Bear Pits was pumped out of a ditch to the top of Monkey Mountain, flowed down a stream, and then through the four pits, three of which were home to Al and two brown bears. Responding to concerns about the lack of clean water for the animals living there, the Parks Department piped in fresh water. But Federal rules on keeping marine mammals, including polar bears, continued to become more and more rigorous, calling for much larger pools and highly filtered water. Bringing even one of the pits up to marine mammal standards would have been impossibly expensive. So the Parks Department officials hoped to bide their time until Al the polar bear died of natural causes. When Jonnie was quite new around the Zoo in the late 1970s, she had not heard that the polar bear's name was Al. The only Al she had met was a zookeeper in the Animal House. He was very nice, a real gentleman, and she was horrified, because she kept hearing the guys from the Parks Department saying that their troubles would all be over, "when Al dies!"

After Al died sometime in the mid-1980s, only two brown bears, a grizzly and a Kodiak, remained in two of the pits. In 1988, the USDA inspector declared that the pits were unfit for these animals, primarily because the water flowed from one pit to the next, a potential for disease transmission. The Parks Department was forced to find a new home for the bears, a nearly impossible task since most legitimate zoos had little room for aged bruins. The only place willing to take them was in Northern Colorado. Concerned about the fate of the bears, the two of us traveled there to see the place for ourselves. We were appalled and sickened! Not only were the cages small, they were filthy. Feces covered the floor, and rotten meat was black with flies. We reported the situation to both the USDA and the Humane Society of the United States. The USDA cited the facility and continued to do so. Government agencies move slowly, however, so the bears were long dead before the place was closed forever. Both of us were dismayed and saddened that we were helpless to change the situation and that these magnificent animals had remained in such deplorable conditions for the rest of their lives. It was one of our saddest experiences at the Zoo.

Grizzly bear in Old Bear Pits during the late 1980s.

(*Image courtesy of the Pueblo Zoological Society*)

Maned Wolves

Since one of the primary objectives of the Pueblo Zoological Society was to participate in conservation programs, Marilyn worked to increase the number of Species Survival Plans represented in the collection. She acquired a pair of maned wolves for the South American Pampas exhibit. Providing the right environment so the animals would breed and raise young proved to be quite a challenge, however. These canines have their pups in the South American summer, our winter, and they prefer to den in seclusion. Giving them privacy was difficult as long as the public could approach the fence along the front side of their exhibit pen. In an attempt to provide the right conditions, zookeepers put up temporary fencing each winter to block off a large area of lawn and path and to prevent approach to the pen. In addition, they had the shelter modified into two dens with a service hallway and added heat mats to the dens.

Their efforts were successful, with the birth of three pups in 2003. Veterinarian Kathy Wolyn and the zookeepers made the hard choice to remove the pups from the den for critical distemper vaccinations. Sadly, this stressed their mother, who injured them. One survived and was named Tega, a shortened version of his father's name, Ortega. After he grew up, Tega was moved to the Denver Zoo.

River Otters

Seeking animals to inhabit the new North American otter exhibit in 2003, Marilyn located a man who had been training two otters to work in the movies. He called them Thelma and Louise. A predator had gotten into their pen, badly injuring both of them. Louise died on the operating table, but Thelma survived, although one of her front legs required amputation. The owner was unsuccessful in finding another companion for Thelma, and when she began showing signs of

Maned wolf.   Maned wolf pup.

(*Images courtesy of the Pueblo Zoological Society*)

aggressive behavior, he sought a new home for her. Area Keeper Melanie Haynes Pococke can best tell the story of how she taught Thelma to swim.

> Thelma came well before the exhibit was finished. She was young and had never been swimming, so I had to work on desensitizing her to the water. She was very afraid of it! I started with mud wallows and baby pools. Eventually, she made circles in small water tubs we provided for her, a huge step, because her feet could not touch the bottom. We had ramps set up in the off-exhibit otter area, which had a large tank. Once, I pushed her into that pool on purpose, which she did not appreciate at all.
>
> After she had been at the Zoo for about three months and was put into the exhibit with its big pool, she cautiously dipped her head under the water and looked around. She found the upper step from the stream into the pool, where she could be submerged, but still able to have her feet on a solid surface. About a week later (and on my day off, to boot) she was playing with a fish in her safe spot, when she found she had floated away from the step. She rushed back, but within minutes a light bulb went on, and she realized she could do it! Fifteen minutes later she was swimming along the bottom of the pool. From then on, she could not seem to stay dry for more than 5 minutes (at least that's what I always said to her).[4]

Before the official opening of the North American river otter exhibit, Marilyn and Melanie picked up two male otters, Thor and Odin, from the ARK Wildlife Rehabilitation in Telluride, Colorado.[5] Watching the three adults otters swim around the pool was a joy. They grew accustomed to the public and seemed to enjoy performing whenever they had an audience. They would playfully follow anyone willing to trot going back and forth in front of the exhibit windows.

---

[4] Melanie Haynes Pococke, personal communication.
[5] Melanie reported that ironically, when the rehab center closed, the former owner wanted to keep one otter as a pet, but state officials insisted she place it elsewhere. That otter's new owner turned out to be the fellow who had given Thelma to the Pueblo Zoo.

Nicole Guarienti playing with river otter Thelma.
(*Image courtesy of Rick Avalos Photography, Pueblo Zoological Society collection*)

Thor eats a fish, while Odin watches.
(*Image by Tammy Guarienti, courtesy of the Pueblo Zoological Society*)

After a couple of years in the exhibit Thelma escaped for a night out. She squeezed through an accidentally unlocked gate at the night pen. One of the Zoo's janitors who worked after closing spotted her and had his partner call Jonnie, who contacted Melanie. While she rushed to the Zoo, the janitor calmly talked to the animal, keeping her entertained until Melanie arrived. His efforts paid off. Thelma was still near the exhibit and easily shepherded back into the pen.

Desert Dan and His Followers

The Zoo received its first camel in 1981. He was an 8-month-old male dromedary from Texas.[6] If the number of articles published by *The Pueblo Chieftain* is any indication, his arrival in the city caused quite a stir. Both Laura Mattoon, at the time Zoological Society Secretary, and Parks Director Lew Quigley were on hand to welcome the young animal. An 11-year-old won a naming contest with her entry of Desert Dan.

Dan lived at the Zoo for many years. Later in life, however, he began having a problem with his pedestal, which is the thick pad on a camel's chest that, when it lies down, raises its body above the hot desert sand and allows air to move underneath. His pedestal had become enlarged, cracked, and bloody—a raw open wound. Over the years, veterinarians examined him and tried various unsuccessful treatments. All agreed that the hard, sometimes very cold ground was the cause. After veterinarian Regis Opferman removed most of the damaged tissue, he called on dermatologist Dr. Kim Dernovsek for help in keeping the area from becoming infected.[7]

Desert Dan wearing a dressing rigged by Dr. Regis Opferman to protect the camel's healing wound.

(*Image courtesy of the Pueblo Zoological Society*)

---

[6] Dromedary camels have one hump (D), while Bactrian camels have two (B). Dromedaries are found on the Arabian Peninsula and in Africa, while Bactrians are from Central and Eastern Asia.

[7] "Dermatologist, Vet Treat Zoo Camel," *The Pueblo Chieftain*, September 14, 1990.

Divali in 2000.
(*Image courtesy of the McBirney Family*)

The wound got some better but did not heal completely. About a year later, it was Dr. Norm Armentrout, who came up with an unlikely treatment: a large, tight rubber band placed around the base of the swollen structure. He left the band in place for several weeks until the huge thing dropped off, leaving the animal's pedestal healed. Unfortunately, scar tissue grew, so in 1992, Norm and Marilyn took Dan to the College of Veterinary Medicine at the Colorado State University in Ft. Collins for surgery to remove this excess tissue. Sadly, Dan died during the surgery from a loss of blood.

After Dan died, Marilyn purchased 19-year-old Wanda from the Tulsa Zoo. Wanda was a dromedary camel that Marilyn had trained while she worked in the children's area of the Houston Zoo. Zookeepers took Wanda for frequent walks and brought her out for several special events. Wanda died in August 1998 from heart failure. During our tenure, there would be other camels: dromedary Mayott, bactrian Divali from the Denver Zoo, and in 1999, Zarafa, a granddaughter of Wanda.

Kangaroos

During the expansion of the Zoo's facilities throughout the 1930s, a variety of animals not native to Colorado were added to the collection. Three kangaroos and an emu from Australia arrived in 1939, sparking significant interest. The way they were acquired was not typical. Traveling to the "land down under" with a letter of request from City Commissioner Ray H. Talbot to the Australian government, famed cowboy Shorty Creede was allowed to keep the kangaroos and emu that he successfully roped in a rodeo. When Creede's ship arrived in the U.S., he found that he lacked clearance permits for the animals. A telegram from Talbot to U. S. Senator Alva Blanchard Adams in Washington D.C. quickly produced the necessary paperwork. Unfortunately, two of the three kangaroos died of dysentery within a month of their arrival in Pueblo.[8]

It would be 1986 before the Zoo would acquire another kangaroo, one that was tragically lost the following year. Others would follow and have such breeding success that by the time the Australian Outback exhibit opened in 1996 the Zoo had its own homegrown mob.

---

[8] "Buckaroo Catches Kangaroo and Emu Too for Local Zoo," and "Pueblo Tough Spot for Baby Kangaroo," The Pueblo Chieftain, May 9 and June 9, 1939, respectively.

Ambassador Conrad and Other Birds

Conrad the Andean Condor was a community favorite. He arrived in 1977 as a surplus animal from the San Francisco Zoo. With his huge 10-foot wingspan, he was a spectacular addition to one of the welded-wire cages near the Zoo entrance. These vultures are the largest flying birds in the world, so interpreting them was an exciting experience for the docents. Every time docent Laura Mattoon came to the Zoo, she immediately headed for Conrad's cage, where he always spread his wings and "danced" for her. In 1992, Conrad was recalled to the San Francisco Zoo, where he would spend his remaining years as a role model for young Andean and California condors. Although the entire community was sad to see him go, for fifteen years he had served the Pueblo Zoo as an ambassador for his species. Conrad died in San Francisco at the age of 40 on October 25, 1999.

We used several birds in education programs, among them a rock pigeon, a screech owl, and a Chihuahuan raven. The rock dove was donated to the Zoo in 1991 by the Psychology Department at Colorado College. Named Rooster, he was quite a character, loving to show off and becoming a long-time star in bird programs.

One of the zookeepers found a screech owl that had been injured by a cat. The veterinarian did what he could, but the little bird was left flightless, one of its wings permanently hanging down. We received federal permission to keep it for use as an animal ambassador and named it Otus (a now outdated genus name for this species). Docent Georgia Lozinsky volunteered to train the owl, working diligently with it on a regular basis.[9] Gradually, Otus became quite docile and able to be handled by several other docents.

Otus the screech owl.

(*Image courtesy of the Pueblo Zoological Society*)

---

[9] Georgia's enthusiasm about animals was contagious. She and her husband, Jim Carsella, operated a web design and hosting business and for many years generously donated these services to the Zoo.

Raven with long-time docent, Anita Bandell.
(*Image courtesy of the Pueblo Zoological Society*)

A young Chihuahuan raven arrived at the Zoo in 1995 from a Texas bird rehabilitator. Given the name Raven, it learned a few words and could perfectly mimic the voices of several of its caretakers. Marilyn and Zoo Educator Mary Tucey fitted it with jesses so it could be put on a leash and taken to programs or outdoors for fresh air.[10] Docent Charlotte Adams often took it outside, where she talked to visitors about this bird of the dry grasslands of the American southwest. On one of these occasions, Raven's leash slipped from her hand, and the bird escaped, flying to the top of the Education Building where it sat making strange noises. It had been in captivity since a chick, so had no chance of survival without human care. While on-lookers gathered, Marti climbed a ladder onto the roof. As she inched slowly higher, Raven inched even higher. Just when she was about to grab its leash, it flew off the roof and landed in a nearby tree. Its frantic squawks led rescuers to it, the leash tangled into the branches of the tree and the big black bird hanging upside down like a big black balloon!

A Raft of Penguins

Once penguin breeding got started in the new Ecocenter exhibit, it continued with gusto. Marilyn served on the Association of Zoos and Aquariums (AZA) African black-footed penguin Species Survival Plan (SSP) committee and was able to obtain several highly ranked pairs for the Zoo. By the time we retired, more than fifty chicks had been hatched and raised successfully. Area

---

[10] Jesses are thin leather straps used to tether a bird while being held or secured on a perch.

Newly hatched African black-footed penguin.

(*Image courtesy of the Pueblo Zoological Society*)

Melanie records the number of fish eaten by each penguin. Vitamins and supplements are concealed inside the fish.

(*Image courtesy of the Pueblo Zoological Society*)

Keeper Melanie Haynes Pococke and other zookeepers carefully monitored the growth of new chicks, eventually taking each one upstairs to an off-exhibit pool where they learned to swim.

The Monsters

Before the Cold-Blooded Creatures herpetarium opened in fall 1986, the City's Senior Zookeeper asked if we could find someone to transport two Gila monsters to Pueblo from a rescue facility in Arizona. Knowing that Sally and Pat Mara were headed in that direction to visit Pat's great aunt, Marti asked them to pick up the rather large and venomous lizards. Two large polystyrene foam containers were loaded into their car, and when Sally questioned the safety of transporting the animals in what looked like flimsy boxes, Marti assured her that they were quite adequate.

After loading up the 2-foot-long reptiles, Sally and Pat headed for Auntie's retirement home and took the boxes inside. To calm her fears, they told her the lizards would be secure in the boxes while they went out for dinner. Upon their return, one of the monsters greeted them with its head poking through a sizeable hole in the container. It was on the verge of escape, having used its sharp claws to dig through the wall of the box. As Sally explains it, Auntie moved quite swiftly to the other side of the room. In fact, she said, they had no idea she could move so quickly. They patched the hole with duct tape, wrapped more tape round and round the boxes, and closed them in their hotel bathroom for the night. They arrived safely in Pueblo, but with quite a tale to tell.

Small Game Hunting

In the spring of 1985, Laura Mattoon and the two of us decided that we needed a kangaroo rat to exhibit in the Discovery Room. So one evening just after dark, we three headed to rural Red Creek Road in Marti's small Datsun. As we drove down the pitch black dark and dusty gravel road with headlights blazing, we saw several of the small rodents run across the road at full tilt. We decided that Jonnie should drive slowly with Laura as spotter in the passenger seat and Marti on the hood of the car grasping a net. It did not take long for Marti to scoop one up. It also did not take long for the poor creature to collapse and die from shock. After that disastrous attempt, it was decided that perhaps a live trap strategically placed in the area might be a better idea. It proved to be successful, as one was caught. It lived for several years in an exhibit that featured this rarely encountered, cute, and ecologically important little prairie animal.

Animals at Home

When the education program was in its infancy, program animals often were kept in homes. Marti relates how a bullsnake, having escaped from its glass aquarium, was found hanging from a clothes hanger in her daughter Christi's closet. Jonnie tells that a large green iguana terrorized a babysitter by descending from the top of a window drape. Docent Christi Sweet, a County high school senior in 1982, kept a young beaver at her family's home until his appetite expanded to include their furniture.

Another animal that lived at the Osborn home was a monkey. Its story begins innocently enough in the summer of 1978. We thought a monkey would be a good addition to the education program, so the Senior Zookeeper found a young male spider monkey. Marti set up a cage in the den of her home.[11] She soon learned she would have to protect the walls behind it with plastic sheeting—otherwise the monkey smeared the walls with everything it could get its hands on (use your imagination). Each day she allowed it to roam around the house under supervision.

After working with it for a few weeks, we decided it was time to try a presentation of the monkey to a classroom full of children. We chose the 4th grade class at Belmont Elementary, attended by Jonnie's youngest daughter and Marti's son. When the day came, Jonnie drove, letting Marti and the monkey out at the far side of the very large and barren schoolyard. Wearing a diaper with a hole for its long tail, the little animal rode on Marti's hip with its arms wound around her neck, just like a baby human. Marti was wearing tall boots, jeans tucked stylishly inside. Tromp, tromp, tromp she strode across the schoolyard. Tromp, tromp, tromp she continued toward the back door of the school. Tromp, tromp, tromp, and then a quick U-turn. Back she came toward the car. What had happened? The smell said it all. No one told us that stressed monkeys have diarrhea. One of Marti's boots was filled to the brim! That was the end of any ideas of monkey presentations. We had learned a valuable lesson—in a very, very, hard way for the monkey and for both of us. This situation is remembered only with the deepest regret.

---

[11] It was not until 2012 that Colorado passed legislation that outlawed private monkey ownership.

Christi Osborn Kurtz is pictured holding the young spider monkey, which was not a good idea, but we were too naïve to realize the dangers to both Christi and the monkey.

(*Image courtesy of Marti Osborn*)

Lessons Learned

A few months after the Society assumed management of the Zoo, when a female beisa oryx was anesthetized for a veterinary procedure, the Zoo did not have fenced runways needed to move the male out of the pen. According to the zookeepers, it happened in a flash. The male walked towards the prone female, moved his head down, and thrust his long horn into her side, puncturing a lung and killing her instantly. The veterinarian and zookeepers, indeed everyone at the Zoo, had received a hard, but valuable lesson about how important it is to have proper animal management facilities. The future would see the addition of much fencing and many gates to assure that all potentially dangerous animals could be separated from zookeepers during daily cleaning and feeding routines or from each other, if necessary.

We learned another lesson, this time from a couple of hedgehogs. Seeking additional animals to use in education programs during the late 1980s, we located a source in New York City that imported African hedgehogs. We ordered two. When they arrived, we received a late evening call that they were waiting for us at the airport. Jonnie took them home for the night. About 2:00 AM, one of them started making a very raspy, hissing sound. Jonnie, who thought something must be terribly wrong, called Marti in a panic, but what could we do in the middle of the night? Checking the encyclopedia in the morning, we learned they were normal sounds made by hedgehogs, often at night. Both males, they probably were not too fond of each other and were very unsure of their new surroundings.

The next morning at the Zoo we noticed that both looked like they had a bad case of dandruff. Veterinarian Regis Opferman checked them over, taking skin scrapings to examine under a microscope. He found mites that were causing mange. Within a couple of days, one of the little animals died, and the other one began losing its spines. Regis searched for a suitable treatment for

Pueblo Zoo's beisa oryx pair in May 1991.

(*Image courtesy of the McBirney Family*)

hedgehogs. Although he had a chart for the appropriate dosages of a parasite-killing drug, it only listed dosages for species from dogs to cattle. There was no recommended dosage for anything as small as this creature. The veterinarian did the best he could, calculated how much might work, crossed his fingers, and gave the poor thing a tiny injection. The hedgehog immediately began to shake violently before falling into a deep sleep, but it didn't die. Nonetheless, it did lose all of its spines and looked very naked and pathetic for over a month. We had learned through this unfortunate experience that sources for the acquisition of animals must be thoroughly vetted. Fortunately, Norman E. Hedgehog would go on to become an ambassador for his species, enjoyed for several years by hundreds of students and Zoo visitors.

Although it is a rather long story, this time we learned a valuable lesson from an animal pro, rather than from an animal. The story began soon after the Society moved to the new education building in 1986, when Jean Sellers came to work part-time as a cashier. That summer she visited her brother in rural Oklahoma and, having heard us wishing for a marsupial, returned to Pueblo with a young Virginia opossum. Her brother had caught it raiding his chicken coop. We were delighted and gave her the honor of naming the animal after her brother, Roy. Since Roy was a male, he did not have a pouch to show, but nevertheless he was a wonderful animal ambassador. He was gentle and willing to put up with multitudes of little hands reaching out to touch him. We had Roy for several years, but unfortunately, no matter how much care they are given, opossums do not live very long. Others would follow: Roger, Polly, and Samantha, among others.

We took Roy to Denver in 1992 for a series of programs with Jim Fowler of *Mutual of Omaha's Wild Kingdom* fame. Although Roy made an appearance at a pre-concert party for Manheim

Jim Fowler holding Roy while Jonnie (*left*) and Marti (*right*) look on.
(*Image courtesy of Marti Osborn*)

Steamroller at Fiddler's Green, it was one of the other animals that gave us trouble. In addition to the opossum, we took a great-horned owl and a six-foot-long boa constrictor in a large, zippered bag. Our job was to hand Jim the animals one-by-one so he could show them to the party guests. All went very well, and since it was a warm evening, after the party we stashed the animals in the car and went inside to enjoy the music.

When the concert ended, we headed to the car only to find the snake bag was empty. After a short search we found the big boa, under the driver's seat, coiled tightly around a heavy metal spring. We could not budge the creature, it was very dark, the parking lot was emptying, and we could not drive the car without risking serious injury to the snake. Panic ensued, but not to worry, Jim Fowler came to our rescue. He gently tapped the snake on the tail, and it immediately began uncoiling itself from the spring. We learned a new trick from a real animal pro.

Returned to Native Habitats

Dr. Ken Danylchuk, a Pueblo orthopedic surgeon and bison rancher, donated several bison to the Lakota Buffalo Caretakers Co-op. Marilyn hoped the Zoo could do the same with four bison calves, in support of the Tribe's efforts to restore the ecology of the northern plains. In 2007, former Puebloan and Executive Director of Village Earth, David Bartecchi, put her in contact with Henry Red Cloud of the Ogallala Sioux Tribe in South Dakota. Arrangements were made for John and Judy Black Feather to travel to Pueblo, give a public presentation at the library, and then transport the animals to their ranch on the Pine Ridge Reservation.

On a warm day in June, Marilyn, several zookeepers, Veterinarian Kathy Wolyn, and Buildings and Grounds Supervisor Jim Pinelle, together with John and Judy Black Feather, herded four half-grown, very strong, and exceedingly rambunctious bison calves into a large horse trailer for the trip to the Black Feathers' Buffalo Ranch on the Pine Ridge Reservation. They were using one of the Zoo's pick-up trucks to "push" the beasts along fenced alleyways toward the trailer. Marti was in the bed of the truck, trying to take photographs. She says, "Whatever possessed me to be there, I'm not sure, because it was anything but a calm event! There was much starting, stopping, turning, and jerking, sometimes with an animal in front of the truck, sometimes with one at the side of the truck. All of it was much less than comforting. Well, actually it was downright scary, because even as juveniles, bison are powerful animals with massive heads and sharp horns." Eventually, the mission was accomplished—all four were in the trailer and headed to South Dakota.

On a couple of other occasions, Pueblo Zoo animals were released in support of conservation programs. A pair of golden eagles raised two chicks that were sent to Kansas to be hacked into their native habitat.[12] The male of the pair was Keesha, who came to the Zoo in December 1980, survived infection with West Nile Virus in 2002, and still was going strong when we retired in 2012.

Another of the Zoo's species that contributed to conservation efforts was the swift fox. Marilyn volunteered to become the Species Survival Plan Swift Fox Coordinator, working to document and track the reproduction of this species under human care. We were fortunate that the Zoo's foxes cooperated with the program, producing a number of offspring. In 2004, six kits were sent to the Cochrane Ecological Institute in Alberta, Canada, where they became part of a breeding program to reintroduce the species, extirpated there since 1928. Although the six would not be released to the wild, their offspring were to be set free on the Canadian prairies.

Swift foxes in their exhibit.
(*Image courtesy of the Pueblo Zoological Society*)

---

[12] Raptors can be released through a process called "hacking," developed as a falconry method to train young birds to hunt. Young are placed in an artificial nest site where they are fed and learn about their environment, gradually learning to fly and hunt. C.G. Jones, "Conservation management of endangered birds," *Bird ecology and conservation: A handbook of techniques*, edited by W.J. Sutherland, I. Newton & R. Green (Oxford: Oxford University Press, 2004), 269-303.

Enrichment might include snowmen for lion Taz Jahari.

(*Image courtesy of the Pueblo Zoological Society*)

Zookeeper Ashley Byers Bowen trains a red panda with a food reward.

(*Image courtesy of the Pueblo Zoological Society*)

Enrichment and Training

Through the years, both the AZA and the USDA have increased their requirements for providing enrichment and behavioral training for animals under human care. While enrichment activities are designed to relieve boredom, trained behaviors through positive reinforcement are designed to aid veterinarians and zookeepers in the safe performance of routine examinations and procedures without the use of anesthetics. Training has become a vital tool in the care of zoo animals.

At the Pueblo Zoo, Marilyn worked with the zookeepers to establish regular enrichment routines. Veterinarian Kathy Wolyn assumed the job of teaching them how to incorporate frequent operant conditioning, positively rewarding desired behaviors with special treats of food, scratching, or brushing.

Animal Collection Goals and Achievements

For many hundreds of years zoos exhibited animals taken directly from the wild. Today animal habitats are rapidly disappearing everywhere in the world, and modern zoos serve as breeding and survival centers for endangered species. The Zoological Society's goals for the Pueblo Zoo were to grow the animal collection only as facilities, staffing, and finances would permit; to move increasingly toward species collectively managed by AZA Species Survival Plans (SSP); and to exhibit and breed minor breeds in the Pioneer Ranch.[13]

---

[13] Minor breeds are rare farm animals that possibly facing extinction.

In 1991, the animal collection was made up of 305 individual animals of 110 species and one domesticated minor breed. Thanks to the work of Marilyn and her staff, by 2012 there were 460 individual animals, representing 136 species, and the number of species managed by SSPs had increased to approximately 33% of the collection. The Pioneer Ranch had become home to Tamworth pigs, and Navajo-Churro sheep, as well as Scotch Highland, Irish Dexter and longhorn cattle.

Chapter Eight

The People

There would be no story to tell about the Pueblo Zoo without the dedication and passion of many, many people. In 1984, the Parks Department and the Zoological Society began to work on plans for the new education building. Some Society members expressed concern that this big improvement was not for the animals. This concern was expressed in a meeting with the architect, who offered this advice, "You will come to understand that it is important to build the human space first." We did indeed discover his statement to be true. Once the Society had space for people to meet, organize, and plan; to benefit from the profits of a small gift shop; and to hold education classes, special events, and fundraisers, things moved faster. People came together to make critically needed improvements for the animals.

The stories of the Zoo's people begin over a hundred years ago. Joe Fritzel Sr. started his career with the City at the Mineral Palace Park caring for "a couple of eagles and owls and bears and a scraggly coyote or two" not long after the turn of the twentieth century. Soon work began on the City Park Zoo, where the first addition was grazing land for a half dozen elk, five mule deer, three buffalo, and several antelope. Joe was named the city's first full-time zookeeper in 1920. Twenty-one year-old William "Bill" Fritzel became his father's assistant in 1929. They worked as a team until Joe's retirement four years later. Louis, another of Joe's sons, started as a gardener in 1935, becoming a zookeeper about ten years later. Bill Fritzel was quoted in an article in *The Pueblo Chieftain* in 1971 as saying, "The birds and animals are fed six days a week. Sunday is the exception, for that is a day visitors toss in more than enough." Bill Fritzel retired in 1972, after 38 years as Head Zoo Keeper."[1]

The story of John Calvin Sutton was only discovered in 2004, about 65 years after the events it describes. When local artist Richard Montano worked to restore the three animal sculptures atop the Animal House cupola, he found a name and date carved into the side of the concrete lion, so he made a rubbing. On December 15, 2005, *The Pueblo Chieftain* ran a copy of the rubbing together with a photograph of Richard and the sculpted lion, in the hope that a reader would

---

[1] "Caring for Zoo Animals Becomes Family Tradition," *The Pueblo Chieftain*, April 6, 1971.

Early zookeepers Bill Fritzell, Homer Buford, and Louis Fritzel pictured in front of two 9'x12' Animal House lion cages.

(*Image courtesy of the Pueblo County Historical Society*)

step forward with new information. Cañon City resident Gil Gillespie responded, identifying the artist as his stepfather, John Sutton. "My stepfather was an old Pueblo boy," he told the paper. He confirmed that Sutton, a self-taught artist, created not only the concrete lion but also the bear and gorilla sculptures atop the building, two monkeys guarding the east door, the seals in the central fountain, the vine-covered drinking fountain, and the bas-reliefs in cages. Sutton later moved to Denver, where at the Denver Zoo he made a wagon pulled by two oxen and completed several other projects in the area. About 1968, Sutton became Curator of Exhibits for the Bronx Zoo in New York, where he created lifelike habitats for the animals. John Sutton died in 1998.[2]

Theodore Pleasant Hamilton, known as "Plessie" to his grandchildren or "T.P." to his coworkers, served as head teamster at City Park from the mid-1930s until horses were no longer used to mow. Thereafter, he worked as a zookeeper and parks foreman until he retired in 1957. His family tells the following story from 1939.

> Plessie never expected problems with the old bull buffalo, but when it turned on him, he jumped the irrigation ditch through the pasture where the small herd of buffalo was kept and ran around a big cottonwood tree a time or two. But, the buffalo caught up with him and tossed him about ten feet in the air alongside the tree. He landed on his head and shoulders,

---

[2] "What's in a Name," and "Zoo Lion Artist Identified," *The Pueblo Chieftain*, December 15 and December 19, 2004, respectively.

Jon Sutton carved JS + BB into the drinking fountain that he decorated with bas-relief.

(*Image courtesy of the Pueblo Zoological Society*)

Theodore Pleasant Hamilton enjoyed showing off the animals, especially lion cubs born at the Pueblo Zoo.

(*Image courtesy of the Hamilton Family*)

breaking his neck. Lying there unconscious with the bull butting him, he would have been gored to death if Louis Fritzel hadn't saved him, endangering his own life in the process. Fritzel pulled a sunflower plant out of the ground along the fence and beat the buffalo off. After wearing a cast for a while, then a leather collar in later years, Hamilton lived an active life to the age of almost eighty.[3]

In summers, the Pueblo Parks and Recreation Department offered various summer jobs to local teens. Jonnie's daughter, Jennifer, tells her experiences working at the Zoo during two summers.

> I was a naïve 16-year-old, hired for my very first job in 1981. I worked as an assistant zookeeper, alongside two other equally inexperienced teenagers. Being raised by a mother interested in animals, I was thrilled to be spending my summer at the Zoo. None of us were trained, we worked unsupervised, and we had full run of the place. What freedom! And, what trouble we got ourselves into! Our jobs included cleaning cages, preparing food, feeding

---

[3] Personal communication, Eugene Hamilton, *Pueblo Zoo Album 1940 - 1970*, Rawlings Library, Pueblo City-County Library District.

animals and keeping unruly visitors at bay. Little did I know what dangerous conditions in which I was working.

Each day, one of my fellow teenagers and I were charged with cleaning the Old Bear Pits. We would arrive at the gate only to be met by a pacing, growling polar bear and his friend, the grizzly. We had morsels of meat that we threw into a small holding pen in the middle of each cage. It took quite a bit of skill and timing to throw the meat, wait for the bear to run into the holding pen, and quickly pull a rope to close an iron gate to keep the animal contained. Then, with the bear clawing furiously at the iron gate, we would shovel the cage.

Cleaning the Old Bear Pits was exhausting work, sometimes in extreme heat, but there was a reward that we secretly waited for each day. The full-time zookeepers gave us the keys to the Zoo and told us to "lock up" at closing time. Three teenagers can have a glorious game of chase on the grounds when left to their own devices. The loser, of course, got quite a dunking as he or she was thrown into the moat surrounding Monkey Island.

But, it wasn't all fun and games, as I would discover when accidents occurred, something for which I was ill equipped. One of the zookeepers had a real love for the most dangerous animals and no fear. He was at the center of several accidents, one involving a beloved Bengal tiger, Doris. She was a beautiful animal, who was by all accounts friendly and loving. This zookeeper had a habit of scratching behind the huge cat's ears as she rubbed against the cage bars. For some unknown reason, one day Doris quickly turned and grabbed his hand. He panicked and pulled his hand from the animal's mouth, in the process severing the area between his middle and ring fingers. [4] I was the only one there with him and panicked myself; however, keeping my wits about me enough to phone 911, help him wrap his hand in a rag, and walk him out to the curb to wait for an ambulance. That apparently was not enough of a warning for him, because it was not much longer until he decided to handle a huge boa constrictor during feeding time. The constrictor, highly alert for food, lurched at him and soon had tightly wrapped all fifteen feet of itself around his arm. Luckily, he had the wherewithal to get himself out of its grasp, because I truly don't know what I would have done. I was no match for a boa constrictor.

It would be years, maybe decades, before I fully confessed to my mother about all the shenanigans that occurred during my summers working at the Zoo.[5]

Through the years we, the authors, would come to know hundreds of volunteers, donors, members, and employees who come to mind as we reminisce. We have included many throughout the book with a few extra stories here. We sincerely apologize for any we may have missed.

One of numerous donors who made the operation and improvement of the Zoo possible was Bob (not Robert!) Johnston. Very much a hands-on gentleman rancher, having grown up on a ranch in San Angelo, Texas, he and his wife, Doris, developed the Red Top Ranch in Southeastern Colorado. We have previously told how Bob spearheaded the building of the Savannah Barn and how he came to our rescue in 1991. He helped again in 1992 after a path had been installed through Happy

---

[4] "Tiger Bites the Hand that Feeds It," *The Pueblo Chieftain*, August 11, 1981.
[5] Jennifer McFarland Whisman, personal communication, 2015.

Time Ranch to provide access to the western part of the Zoo. A bridge over the ditch (canal) in the northwest corner was needed so visitors could walk from the hoofstock pens to the Animal House without having to double back. As soon as Bob heard the idea of building a bridge, he got right on it, talking the owners of a local business out of several huge precast concrete spans and hiring a crane to place them over the water. Within a few weeks, the Zoo had "Bob's Bridge." Bob became a Society Board member and a special friend, remaining a supporter of the Zoo until his death in 2005.

Friends and acquaintances often dropped into our offices. One who particularly comes to mind was a great guy, although perhaps a bit eccentric. Red, a cowboy much of his adult life, was retired and lived in a very big, quite old warehouse, surrounded by his extensive collection of all kinds of mechanical things and vehicles. Since he lived in a prairie habitat in a place with lots of nooks and crannies, interesting creatures often crawled into his view. He would put them into a variety of jars and bring them to us. It might be a scorpion, a centipede, a beetle, a spider. He loved having us identify the critters and hoped we would use them in displays, which we often did.

There were some employees who remained with us from 1991, when the City turned over the Zoo to the Society, until our retirements in 2012. One of the first five zookeepers hired by the Society, Melanie Haynes Pococke, continued to work at the Zoo for almost 25 years. Carl Ecker was a part-time employee of the Parks Department who stayed on until long after the two of us had retired. As a farm keeper in charge of the chickens, rabbits, turkeys and other animals, he provided much needed consistency in animal care. A favorite of the rest of the staff, Carl loved his job and was always willing to take on extra tasks and new challenges.

Carl Ecker at work in the Pioneer Ranch.

(*Image courtesy of the Pueblo Zoological Society*)

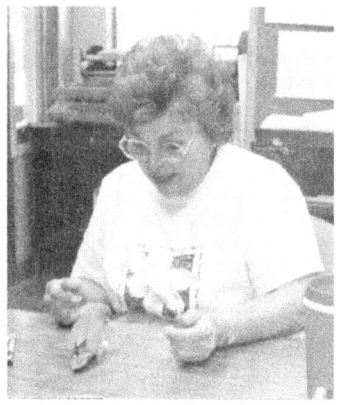

Betty Kolesarek with her pal, Gregory the lovebird.

(*Image courtesy of the Pueblo Zoological Society*)

Nina Chimento.

(*Image courtesy of the Chimento family*)

Jeanette Ball.

(*Image courtesy of Marti Osborn*)

Betty Kolesarek started work as a Zoo cashier for the Parks Department soon after the Education Building was completed in 1986. In 1991, she continued as a cashier and became the Society's bookkeeper. She was a special lady with a contagious laughter and outgoing personality. Not only did she have a way with people, she also related quite well to birds. One of them, Gregory the lovebird, did not respond favorably to most of us, but Betty was a different story. She would take him out of his cage and let him wander on her desk, where he was quite happy. Betty's time with us was cut short when she died very unexpectedly on March 1, 2003.

In the late 1980s, the Parks Department hired Nina Chimento as a Zoo cashier. When the management changed, Nina could have moved into another City position, but she was willing to take a chance with us. She stayed at the Zoo until after we retired, for a total of 23 years. Nina was in charge of finding and scheduling gift shop volunteers, making calls to schedule and remind docents, arranging monthly docent luncheons, and managing membership correspondence and data entry, all while she greeted visitors at the admission window. As the Zoo grew, other cashiers were hired, including long-time employees Jeanette Ball, Nancy Lamas, Janice Martinez, and Vivian Espinosa.

Two very important sources of earned revenue for the Zoo are the food concession and the gift shop. A contracted concessionaire operated the Watering Hole snack bar after it opened in 1994. But realizing the Society could earn more by controlling the operation, the contract was terminated after only a couple of years. Verona Miller, a docent and a part-time cashier, was hired as manager in about 1995, a position she held until she her unexpected death in 2010. After that a local restaurateur took over the operation.

Retired teacher Betty Wilkinson began volunteering as a Zoo Docent and in the Zoovenir Shop in 1983. She soon became the unpaid manager, a position for which she was well suited, since she loved to shop. Spending someone else's money made it even better! During the authors' years at the Zoo, the gift shop was staffed primarily by volunteers, including Charlene Gardner, Mary Beck, Hannah Gibbs, Arlene Alderton, Annie VanBeuren, and Laura Schwager, to mention just a few who worked there the longest. When Betty began thinking about retirement, she started training her replacement, Carol Ecker.

At first the Society could not afford employees assigned specifically to marketing, events management, or development. The two of us handled those areas ourselves until the job grew too big. Our first Marketing and Events Coordinator was Tracey Mattoon, who got things started and stayed with us for a couple of years. Pat Ponce then came onboard, first as Marketing and Events Coordinator, but once we could afford more help, she became Development Assistant, and in that position she was in large part responsible for raising the $3.2 million for Islands of Life. Elaine Zavislan then filled the Marketing and Events Coordinator position. After her retirement, Jackie Bernal assumed the position. Next came soft-spoken Jan Goldman, who loved all of Earth's creatures, often sharing her office with one or more of the education animals. Jen Myers, Linda Frakes, Gloria Madrill, and Vikki Graston would follow to fill jobs largely invented by their predecessors.

We have no doubt omitted many outstanding zookeepers. Most remained at the Zoo for only a few years, however. Small zoos like the one in Pueblo often are career stepping stones for zookeepers, leading to employment at larger zoos or advancements in their careers. Some long-time animal care employees who stayed with the Society for many years include Heather Smith, Kim Cooper Pranger, Ashley Byers Bowen, Zeb Clayton, and Nikki Emanuel.

It goes without saying that a zoo must have zookeepers, but it may not be quite as obvious that there must be many others working behind-the-scenes to keep everything running smoothly. One of the Society's earliest hires for the Zoo was Chuck Johnston, a retiree

Carol Ecker in the Zoo's gift shop.

(*Image courtesy of John Alderton*)

Jan Goldman with a barn owl.

(*Image courtesy of*
The Pueblo Chieftain)

Zeb Clayton, shown here with Zeb Junior, was a ZooCrew member hired as a zookeeper after high school graduation. When a kid goat was rejected by its mother, Zeb took on its care, and his fellow zookeepers named it after him.

(*Image courtesy of the Pueblo Zoological Society*)

John Alderton repairing an irrigation line, a never-ending challenge.

(*Image courtesy of the Pueblo Zoological Society*)

with extensive experience in every imaginable buildings and grounds area. From the beginning, Chuck needed a place to work, so he singlehandedly tackled a small outbuilding that he called "The Shop." It was filled with useless junk and had been partially burned sometime in its long history, but Chuck was up to the challenge and produced a decent place for his building and repair projects.

After Chuck left in 1994, Dan Carty took over for a few years. Then in 1998, Jim Pinelle was hired. Another person with a great deal of experience in many areas, he soon learned about the equipment necessary to run seven major buildings, many smaller structures, and 25 acres of grounds. John Alderton joined the maintenance crew in 2000, experienced in many areas of maintenance including irrigation systems. His ready sense of humor was an added benefit.[6] As the staff person in charge of the ElectriCritters holiday lighting event, he designed the show layout, ordered supplies, and supervised installation and teardown. When it became necessary to have more help in caring for increased landscaping, Lynn Peterson and Richard Valdez, both retired from other careers, came on board. Lynn signed on as a gardener but soon found himself assigned many other tasks. Richard asked that we keep him busy, a request he may have regretted.

The Society hired horticulturist Karen Adams to enhance the Zoo's well-manicured lawns dotted with mature trees by adding new plantings and gardens. At the lion exhibit she won several awards for plantings that closely resembled the African habitat of the animals. Despite the challenges presented by gardening in a semi-arid environment and with limited staff, the Society continued to add gardens. The Woods was transformed from bare ground into a lush forest, and major landscaping projects were accomplished at the Pioneer Ranch, Grasslands of

---

[6] Without the help of Parks Department employee Mike Johnson, we would have been at a loss to locate existing irrigation lines, valves, and connections.

the World, otter exhibit, and Islands of Life. Specialty gardens included annual, rock, perennial, pollination, and cactus. After Karen's untimely death in 2002, horticulture was added to Marti's responsibilities. This expansion of Marti's duties necessitated the hiring of part-time Education Assistants, including Avaril Woodward, Mary Tucey, Kay Keen, and Sue Hardesty. Volunteer Carol Ann Moore-Ede also served as an education assistant for about five years.

Economically operating a fairly large facility meant that volunteers were critical in supplementing the work of the Society's staff. Useful Public Service workers were assigned to work at the Zoo and Colorado Department of Corrections female inmates did grounds work under the supervision of corrections officers. Many groups from organizations or companies volunteered to help with special projects. Individuals volunteered as docents, animal care assistants, gardeners, and special events crew.

Lynn Peterson and Richard Valdez.

(*Image courtesy of John Alderton*)

Some volunteers started in the 1980s and stayed with us throughout our time at the Zoo. Among them are Linda Stefanic, Laura Mattoon, Art Schwager, and Charlotte Adams. Linda was a Zoo Docent, as well as Board of Directors President and an always willing volunteer. Even when things were not going well, Linda could be counted upon to calmly assure us that things would move forward, despite obstacles and setbacks.

An article published on April 16, 1981 in *The Pueblo Chieftain* and entitled "Labor of Love" described a large stained glass window made and donated for installation in the Animal House by Laura Mattoon. Laura was a docent, a Board President, Zoofari Chair, and a dedicated supporter for the remainder of her life. She was a gutsy lady whose tenacity resulted in many improvements. She remained a dear friend and ally until illness took her from us.

Volunteer Art Schwager was an essential part of the small crew that installed the first Discovery Room displays. Art was a docent as well as the go-to-guy for anything that needed to be fixed. Over many years he made a pictorial and video history of all new exhibits and events. The capital campaign for the Ecocenter included a school donation program, "Pennies for Penguins." The thousands of dollars raised were extremely heavy in the form of pennies, and it was Art who lugged them from schools to the bank. Self-described as "one of the girls," he enthusiastically represented the Zoo everywhere he went and only ill health ended his time at the Zoo.

Charlotte Adams continued volunteering at the Zoo long after the two of us retired. Passionate about animals, she was a perfect caretaker for the ones in the education collection. She showed animals at virtually every special event and made presentations in the Discovery Room. Charlotte's

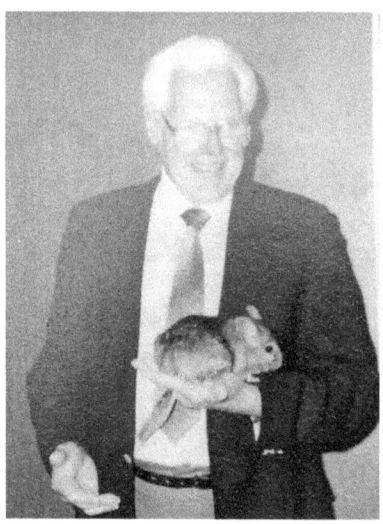

Art Schwager holding
a chinchilla.

(*Image courtesy of the
Pueblo Zoological Society*)

Charlotte Adams and
a fantailed pigeon.

(*Image courtesy of the Pueblo
Zoological Society*)

dedication, faithfulness, and cheerful personality were unmatched and so appreciated—most especially by the animals in her charge.

Marilyn McBirney

Hiring a curator to be in charge of the Zoo's animal operations was nearly at the top of our TO DO list as we prepared to assume management of the facility in the final two months of 1990. We advertised nationally though the American Association of Zoos and Aquariums and received numerous applications. As we narrowed the field, we brought two candidates to Pueblo for interviews that included tours of the Zoo and community and social events with Board members. Much to our dismay, these two just did not seem to be a good fit with the organization. We were at wits end when we received a late application, more than a few days after the deadline. The applicant sounded interesting. She had started her career at the Houston Zoo as a teenage volunteer and progressed to supervisor of the children's zoo. A phone call revealed that she was about to travel to Colorado for a vacation and was available to make a stop in Pueblo for an interview. The two of us, together with a few Board members, took her to lunch. By that time, we were worn out, so, there were no tours, no social events, just lunch. But conversation over lunch was enough. Marilyn McBirney was offered and accepted the position the next day. The rest became history. By February 1991 she had moved to Pueblo, and she stayed at the Zoo for the next 23 years.

Marilyn's work was critical in helping us achieve the Zoo's first accreditation, as well as in the development of all the exhibits built or remodeled from 1991 through 2012. Chair of the Swift Fox Species Survival Plan and a member of the African Penguin SSP, she guided the Pueblo Zoo's participation in numerous conservation programs. She deserved much of the credit for making Islands of Life a success. She chose animals with the goal of emptying the building before demolition in 1999, she selected new species and secured them for the exhibits, she helped design the animal enclosures, and she watched over every aspect of construction. Without her extensive knowledge of animals and their behaviors, Islands of Life would not have become a reality. In the words of a long-time zookeeper, "You knew Marilyn cared about everyone and every animal. She cared so much. You never could question her commitment. Her own life took second place to the needs of the Zoo."

Unfortunately, her employment at the Pueblo Zoo was terminated in January 2014 by Jonnie's successor, after which she became General Curator at the Abilene Zoo in Texas. Not long after she arrived there, she tragically passed away, following a battle with cancer.

Said Marilyn, "I consider myself lucky that I get to do what I truly enjoy for a living."[7]

Marilyn McBirney holding a great horned owl.

(*Image courtesy of the Pueblo Zoological Society*)

---

[7] "For Marilyn McBirney, Life is a Zoo," *The Pueblo Chieftain*, February 24, 1994.

Jim Pinelle

One of the people instrumental in the successful operation of the Zoo and a member of our senior staff, Buildings and Grounds Supervisor Jim Pinelle seemed always to be able to fix things: the penguin filtration system, aged trucks, heat pumps, HVAC systems, and the list goes on. He could talk folks into giving the Zoo really good deals on purchases or into free labor or into donating tires, transformers, and loads of dirt. He was the Zoo's project manager on construction projects, be they large or small. He no doubt knows the location of every water, gas, and electrical line on the property. Always practical and analytical in his thinking, he contributed a great deal to the exhibit planning process, as well as to day-to-day operations. His expertise and ability have been critical to the development of the Zoo.

Jim Pinelle on the Zoo's tractor.

(*Image courtesy of the Pueblo Zoological Society*)

Richard Montano

Richard Montano graduated from the former University of Southern Colorado (now Colorado State University–Pueblo) with degrees in both civil engineering and art and was introduced to us in 1982 by a city planner as someone who might be able to draw a map of the Zoo. After completing the map, he produced the Zoo's first real interpretive sign, and then a second one, and then he drew a new logo for the organization. In 1985, he designed and fabricated most of the exhibits in the Mahlon T. White Discovery Room, and in 1986 he designed the reptile habitats for the Cold-Blooded Creatures herpetarium, building the diorama. After that, we lost count, but we had learned how very versatile his skills were and began to call on him more and more.

Richard Montano in a 2002.

(*Image courtesy of* The Pueblo Chieftain)

Richard worked on every new exhibit, every new sign, every exhibit challenge, every event logo, every donor recognition, and every ElectriCritters animal figure. There truly is no way to thank Richard enough for giving his talents and his heart to the Pueblo Zoo.

"It's nice to be able to do things that are seen by the whole community—it kind of gives you a special satisfaction," said Richard Montano.[8]

---

[8] "Animal Instinct," *The Pueblo Chieftain*, July 28, 2002.

Epilogue

Retirement and Final Thoughts

As the end of 2011 and our announced retirements approached, we realized we were not quite ready. A new Executive Director had not yet been hired, and the deadline for submission of accreditation materials was upon us. We moved our final days of work into July 2012 and headed into six months that seem a bit of a blur to both of us. The capital campaign to build the black rhino exhibit and wildlife learning center continued. Marti worked closely with Sue Hardesty, who had been chosen to fill her position. We both worked with the Transition Team, conducting interviews for the Executive Director position. The rest of the staff toiled at getting the Zoo ready for its accreditation inspection in June. It was a sad time to be leaving all we had worked so hard on for thirty-six years. But it also was an exciting time to learn how much the community appreciated the transformation of the Zoo into a facility of which they could so rightfully be proud. It was a time for us to reflect on how thankful we were for the help and support of countless others: Board members and government officials willing to take a risk on the future and employees who always went the extra mile for a place they loved, as well as volunteers and donors, without whom the Zoo could not possibly have survived.

Mike Blazer, Zoological Society President in 2011, summed up the work to be done as follows:

> Possibly the largest initiative taken on by the Board of Directors in 2011 was the implementation of a Transition Team to start the search for a new Executive Director. Comprised of the present Executive Committee, along with a number of zoo board past presidents, the planning was put in place to develop a process that would secure the hiring of Senior Staff to carry on the legacy that Jonnie and Marti fostered over the last 21 years. To make these tasks even more challenging, the above was accomplished on a budget that continually gets strained by ever increasing costs and economic variables. Even so, the Pueblo Zoo continues to improve and build for the future.[1]

Upon our retirements in July 2012, we were honored at the annual Zoofari, by friends and associates at a picnic in the Mandari, and by Board and staff at a barbeque hosted by Sally Mara

---

[1] *Pueblo Zoological Society 2011 Annual Report,* Pueblo Zoo, page 1.

and Carol Rickman. At this final event, each of us was given a plaque that included a bronze relief sculpture, a small-scale replica of the lion head that adorns the brick pillar at the west entrance to Pueblo's City Park.

We left our successors with a long list of challenges to face in the future. A growing animal collection would require more animal care staff. More landscaping and more buildings would require maintenance. Accreditation would be more rigorous. We did not have time to face what to do with the historic Old Bear Pits and Monkey Mountain. It was time for new leadership and enthusiasm, but hard to leave with so much more to be done and so many wonderful people left behind.

A City Manager once said he could bus everyone living in Pueblo to the Cheyenne Mountain Zoo at less cost than maintaining a zoo in our small town. Yet, on the day that a new and spectacular lion exhibit opened at the Cheyenne Mountain Zoo, a reporter asked a youngster who was peering through the glass at one of the huge cats whether he had ever seen a lion so close before. Without hesitation the little boy said, "Sure, at the Pueblo Zoo."

Appendix A

Pueblo Zoological Society
Board of Directors Presidents
1976 to 2012

During our tenure, the Pueblo Zoological Society grew and prospered on the strength of its leaders. The following gave generously of their time, talents, and treasure. We give heartfelt thanks and admiration to this group of dedicated individuals.

Dan Gill 1976
Ed Lane 1977-1979
Joe Saunders (interim) 1979
Margaret Crader 1979-1980
Marti Osborn 1980-1981
Jonnene McFarland 1981
Laura Mattoon, 1982-1983
Linda Stefanic 1983-1985
Karen Adams, 1985-1986
Art Schwager, 1987-1989
Catherine Spangler, 1989-1991
Bill Brill, 1991-1993
Corinne Koehler 1993
Kathrine Thomson, 1994-1995
Ron Velarde, 1996-1997
Sally Mara 1998-1999
Colennda Fratterelli 2000-2002
Larry G. Moore 2002-2004
Linda Stefanic 2005
Carol Rickman 2006-2007
John Ercul 2008-2009
Mike Blazer 2010-2011
Karen Ross 2012

Appendix B

Pueblo Zoo Veterinarians
Early 1900s through 2012

The veterinary staff plays a special role at any zoo, not only mending and curing ailing animals of all sorts and sizes, but also recommending diets, housing, and husbandry. They must have an enthusiasm for learning, because their patient may be a lion one day, a snake the next. From almost the very beginning to the end of our years of involvement, the Pueblo Zoo benefited from the knowledge and caring of six special individuals.

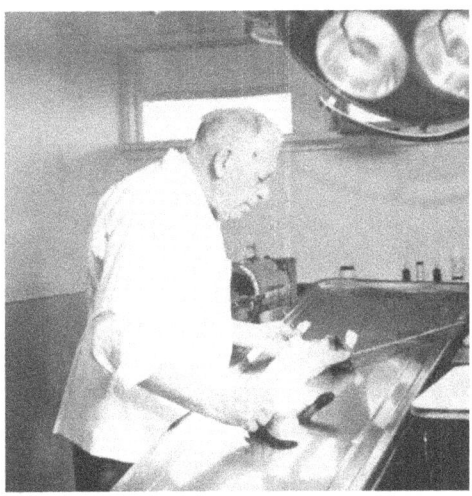

Arthur Neale Carroll, DVM (1891-1976)
Pueblo Zoo Veterinarian early-1900s to mid-1940s.

(Image courtesy of the Carroll Family)

Walter Dana "Butch" Carroll, DVM (1922-1994)
Pueblo Zoo Veterinarian 1946 to 1980.

(*Image courtesy of the Carroll Family*)

Regis Opeferman, DVM
Pueblo Zoo Veterinarian 1980 to 1992.

(*Image courtesy of Pueblo Zoological Society*)

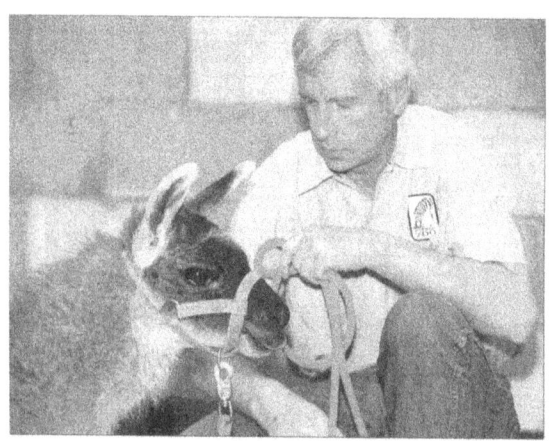

Norm Armentrout, DVM
Pueblo Zoo Veterinarian 1992 to 2003.

(*Image courtesy of* The Pueblo Chieftain)

Kathy Wolyn, DVM
Pueblo Zoo Veterinarian 2003 to present.

(*Image courtest of the Pueblo Zoological Society*)

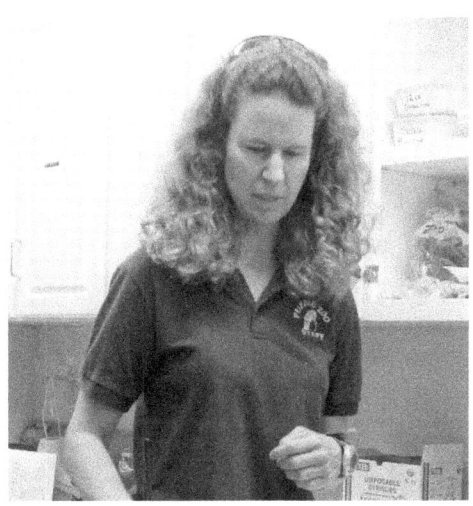

Kim Cooper Pranger, CVT,
Pueblo Zoo Veterinary Technician 1999 to present.

(*Image courtest of the Pueblo Zoological Society*)

Appendix C

Tribute to Marilyn McBirney

A Letter to the Editor published in *The Pueblo Chieftain* on February 1, 2014:

When we retired from the Pueblo Zoo almost 2 years ago, we were honored at parties, given gifts, and praised in a *Chieftain* article. Now, as Marilyn McBirney moves on to a new phase in her career, we feel she, too, should be honored for her accomplishments on behalf of the Pueblo community. Without her help, there would have been little reason to honor us!

Marilyn worked with us in the position of General Curator/Conservation Manager for nearly 21 years—from February 1991 until our retirements in July 2012. When the Zoological Society assumed management of the zoo in 1991, the facility was was in danger of being closed because it was out of compliance with the USDA Animal Welfare regulations. However, with the vital assistance of Marilyn, within a just a little over one year the zoo was not only brought into compliance with these regulations, but also was accredited by the American Association of Zoological Parks and Aquariums.

As soon as Marilyn came on board, she took on the training of our early keepers, many of whom had minimal experience and little knowledge of the zoo world. Several of those she trained through the years have moved on to larger zoos. Others remain at the Pueblo Zoo, providing excellent care for the animals and helping with successful breeding programs, developed by Marilyn.

Marilyn is an exceptionally dedicated professional, having developed her career from teen volunteer through curation of the Pueblo Zoo's diverse animal collection. Her natural curiosity causes her to ask questions about absolutely everything—that is what makes her such a good animal curator! Many likely do not realize the knowledge and skill it takes to successfully care for such a wide range of animals. Each species behaves differently, eats different things, has different reproductive strategies, requires different lighting, etc. And, because she built a good reputation in the zoo industry for the Pueblo Zoo's animal care program, she was able to acquire many new species of animals, including several valuable breeding pairs. For example, under her direction, the zoo's penguins have produced almost 60 chicks since 1992, and in 2013 the maned wolves gave birth to two of the only four pups born during the year in the United States. In addition, she oversaw participation in many Species Survival Plans and was the coordinator for the swift fox program.

Familiar with all aspects of the zoo, Marilyn worked closely with operations staff in accomplishing maintenance and improvement projects. Because of her knowledge of animals and their behaviors, her skills in exhibit planning are outstanding and the main reason all of the Pueblo Zoo's new exhibits are so successful. As the staff worked with zoo designers in developing plans, it was Marilyn who either knew or researched what was needed to accommodate the variety of animals in the exhibits—from exactly where drains were placed to exhibit sizes, fencing materials to be used, and enrichment items needed to prevent animal boredom. Sometimes she "drove us up a wall" with her insistence on including features that we thought unnecessary, but which she saw as crucial for management of the animals. One example of this is the large off-exhibit area provided for the river otters. We thought she was asking for too much area. But recently, the Reed/Smith North American River Otter Husbandry Guide highlighted the Pueblo Zoo's as one of the best otter exhibits in North America, primarily because of this large holding area. During the time that we worked together, millions of dollars in capital improvements were made to the facility. If you enjoy the zoo, you must realize that success of the the African lion, African penguin, rainforest, Asian Adventure, World of Color, Islands of Life, Pioneer Ranch, and the North American river ottter exhibits were in great part due to the expertise of Marilyn.

Marilyn was the "go to" person, if you had a question about any animal. Consequently, she worked well with the Education Department and docents, providing valuable information for exhibit signs and newspaper articles.

Although we sometimes had our differences, we were all part of a team, working to make the Pueblo Zoo better—even on a ridiculously small budget. Bringing the zoo from the brink of closure to its current excellence, required hundreds of people—donors, government officials, volunteers, staff, architects and contractors . . . the list goes on. But it also required a person with the expertise and dedication found in Marilyn McBirney.

We are sure that we are not alone in wishing to thank Marilyn and wish her the very best in her future endeavors.

Jonnene McFarland
Director, Pueblo Zoo/Pueblo Zoological Society, Retired

Marti Osborn
Associate Director/Education & Horticulture, Pueblo Zoo/Pueblo Zoological Society, Retired

www.ingramcontent.com/pod-product-compliance
Lightning Source LLC
Chambersburg PA
CBHW080848020526
44118CB00037B/2318